PURGING MATTERS

PAUL GAASENBEEK

iUniverse, Inc.
Bloomington

Purging Matters

iUniverse books may be ordered through booksellers or by contacting:

iUniverse
1663 Liberty Drive
Bloomington, IN 47403
www.iuniverse.com
1-800-Authors (1-800-288-4677)

Because of the dynamic nature of the Internet, any web addresses or links contained in this book may have changed since publication and may no longer be valid. The views expressed in this work are solely those of the author and do not necessarily reflect the views of the publisher, and the publisher hereby disclaims any responsibility for them.

Any people depicted in stock imagery provided by Thinkstock are models, and such images are being used for illustrative purposes only.

Certain stock imagery © Thinkstock.

ISBN: 978-1-4620-6076-4 (sc)
ISBN: 978-1-4620-6078-8 (e)
ISBN: 978-1-4620-6077-1 (dj)

Library of Congress Control Number: 2011918458

Printed in the United States of America

iUniverse rev. date: 04/27/2012

TABLE OF CONTENTS

Part 3 - The End

PURGING MATTERS

THE HAUNTING DARKNESS OF my mind engulfs my reality, blinding my vision from the truth I do not know but desperately seek to see. Amazingly, while I wrestle with my sight, I am still able to run from my nightmare and towards what I hope will be a light. I manically manage to do so thanks to my nervous system reminding my brain that I do not want to die. The fight or flight response has taken over for my fragile and confused mind—a psyche that is long gone.

As I scuttle about, my dead spirit and dying body clings pathetically to life like a lowly, deformed frog trying to survive an environmental disaster—a tripod, or three legged frog if you will, that "thinks" it is one bad leap away from being grotesquely consumed by what lurks within its rented cesspool of life. The life alarm is ringing loudly, but sadly no one can hear the warning. So like the sad, little, anonymous frog and without thought, I keep up the endless struggle to survive my untenable life by staying just one small step ahead of my monstrous maker.

While I am scurrying rabidly and into obscurity, the sound of my breathing, my existence, is lost into the stagnant air and ominous quiet. Life, ironically an exaggeration of reality, passes me by painfully slowly—like a kidney stone or an episode of any television show loaded with pointed commercials that warp my good senses (just about all of them these days). I am alone. My dream is my fate.

I quickly peer behind me as another cold dagger of sweat begins to form on my pale skin. Death is nearer now, as a tidal wave of fear hangs precariously above me, readying to bring my life to its inevitable end. *This is it for me* my anxious body screams as I am showered with fear. There is no escaping this all too real nightmare.

Please stop! I don't want to die! I don't want to die, I cry out pathetically and predictably into deaf ears anyway. No one can save me—well, except for maybe me, but I don't have time to think about that now, as I am too busy running. I start to weep as my quivering body and I hurry off and into one of the deepest caverns of my vacuous intellect. It is time to hang on, as the giant wave of trepidation is almost here; five, four, three, two, one...

"It is now time for the morning weather report from our whacky Jack Frost."

"Thank you, Mary. Good news for those who are commuting to work today; it is crazy cold out there this morning, and the roads are as slippery as murderers who go on trial in Los Angeles— and apparently Florida as well. Top that guilt-free cake off with a balmy high of two degrees, and you have yourself the makings of a delicious day. Buckle up like OJ had to, people, because you can run but you cannot hide; winter is here! Now back to the morning news."

BANG!

Shut it, you too-ugly-for-television dick jockey" I think to myself.

Damn! What a way to start the week. I have literally just woken up, and I already feel frazzled to the gills. If I was a fish, I would be drowning faster than my readers are putting down this book. And that dream? What the hell? What was I running from? Whoever or whatever the boogie man was, it seemed way too real for my liking. Sigh! Please give me a generous minute, as I need to catch up with my runaway mind. I curl up into as small a ball as my round stomach allows me to and start to cry quietly.

My Morning at Home

AS I LAY HERE in bed with my heart racing like an eighty-year-old, used-to-be-male on Viagra—irregular, fast, and just plain scary—I quicken the need for a quadruple bypass by stressing about activities like styling my hair, plucking my eye brows, and shaving. It is weird how my impending heart attack seems to have everything to do with my excess body hair. Yes, I am being a little dramatic, but this is a sign of how stressed out and miserable I am. However, even when on vacation, I am constantly mindful about spending too much money, so there appears to be absolutely no decompression time for me in my adult life. It feels like I am always busy suckling from the tit of life—my socialization, in some mindless way—and this is making me sick. I labor hard so I can enjoy my existence to a degree, but at every breast, I get a mammogram instead of milk so my anger and stress levels are growing. My existence really sucks because of all the examinations and lack of anxiety-free moments. From A to Z—anxiety to Zoloft—the spectrum is complete.

I am getting this information out of the way right now so you don't assume I am merely having a wretched emergence to this miraculous, yet dark dawning of a new week. So there you have it; welcome to my crummy life. I hope to catch my runaway-thinking train soon, but for now I need to keep on running in the direction of work. My brain may be derailed, but at least I still have my health. Whoa, that was a weird pain!

So, for better or for worse, here I am at seven thirty-three on a Monday morning already wishing it was Friday at seven when it is okay to leave work and not look like a piker. On top of feeling like a fish in a bowl that is looking into the used barrel of a hunter's gun,

I feel like I did not even sleep a wink last night.

As an aside, I don't get what constitutes nighttime? Should people say I slept one hour last night and seven this morning if they went to bed at eleven? Does this make sense? Does anyone even care? Humor me for a while, as my bed is nice and warm and I do not feel like moving. There is a method to my madness you know.

Anyway, as I try to ascend from my melancholic slumber, I can't help but feel warm, comfortable, and safe. I don't want to move, never mind get up. I close my eyes and think that I am enjoying the moment...

"What you need to do is stay warm. It is a cold one out there today."

BANG! BANG! BANG!

"And stay dead," I holler!

It is now eight-thirty. I peel my round behind out of bed quicker than a newly elected politician—incredibly and ironically accomplished on his first day at work while repeating the oath of office—breaks his platform promise to work on behalf of the people and to bring credibility back to politics. Anyway, it is time to start my morning ritual. First on my mental list of things to do is thinking about what number two is—which is pondering number three. Momentum, my friend, is the key to everything.

With the first couple of tasks completed, I do move on to rung number three, and that is to contemplate the following: Why am I living like this? I hate my profession to be sure, but more importantly, I am entertaining a relationship with myself that is so dysfunctional it makes politicians on every side of the aisle look like best of friends. Read into that as you wish. I was granted the right to live at birth, but if surviving constitutes living to those who made the rules, then let's do things right; paint me red, white, and green; hang me up; and call me a human piñata. Look up the history of the piñata if you want to understand that. The reference is very apt, to say the least. Anyway, it is time to move on to the next step—the shower—as I do not have time to think about anything else on my sad, little list now. Of course, I never do. Excuse me, please.

I jump into the shower with a heart rate of about 150 beats per second. That extra hour of sleep has really paid off for me, as now I can die from cardiac arrest well rested. Where is that damn phone?

"Nine-one-one. What's the emergency?"

Nothing is going right for me. Even my grammar sucks, right? Well, as long as you can understand me I am okay with that. Truly, having "impeccable" grammar is the least of my worries right now; this is a book of ideas and not grammar. Thus, I will continue to make mistakes on purpose just to prove that point. Does this cover me from being liable; like every company around that puts lame warning labels on their products just in case?

You should read what some companies are sticking on their products these days. Don't stop the chainsaw with your hands. Don't spray the Windex in your eyes. Keep the baby oil away from babies. This Superman cape cannot make you fly. These are all real warning labels that have been plastered on products in our world. The winner of course is from dry cleaners who claim they are not responsible for what happens to our garments after they agree to take them. There is no more suing for coffee that is too hot either in a lateral move of thought. Now, also true is not getting on writers for poor grammar and content. Yes, I just said that but I have a sign so all good.

Wow, this shampoo is really burning my eyes today. Oh my goodness, it is soap! As I blast the tiny bubbles from my irritated eyeballs using water that can't make up its mind if it wants to be way to hot or cold, all I can think about during my "morning moment of reflection" is what a terrific start of the new week this is turning out to be. I could not have planned it any better. This "moment" is step six of my habitual morning ritual. I deleted step five for you, as that is just me swearing and shouting uncontrollably for as long as I feel I need to.

After my pseudo like shower, I feed my cat with one chubby stump still naked of its made-for-a-model pant leg and then quickly eat my breakfast, which at home is nothing more than a golden brown three-week-old banana. Yes, bananas are supposed to be yellow; but when first picked they are actually green. The bananas are then gassed with ethylene in order to quicken the ripening process to turn them yellow. Finally, due to the bananas sitting out forever, they turn brown like mine. Provocative information or what? Next I am going to talk about how hair grows. Anyway, enough about produce or anything else, for that matter, as I really need to get my clogged arteries out of here and fast.

So, that was my glorious morning at home. I would prefer it to be more peaceful and not like being at a Slayer concert, but things always could be worse. So for now, out the all too thin societal storm blocking door I go. And "storm blocking" because my home is my castle and no one can get me here, right?

Looking back, though, I think I filled Babo's food bowl with some kind of delicious and supposedly nutritious cereal. Cats eat anything and everything, don't they? I feel bad for poor Babo. I will make things up to my cute, little kitty later. Sadly, if I had a nickel for every time I uttered those empty words I would be a few more dollars in debt after factoring in those shifty, little bank fees and, of course, inflation.

Now there is one thing you should be aware of before we move forward. I go off on some of the same things from time to time, but please look at the title of this book. If I was not constantly purging—sharing my feelings about what I see and think (either that or talking about bulimia)-wouldn't you start to wonder why the hell this is book called, *Purging Matters?* I feverishly and honestly attack all that is wrong in society—everything— and I make no excuses for this. I enjoy feeling free, so I don't hold back saying what is on my mind. Now, it may seem like I vent like a volcano in Hawaii—all the time and without thought—but hidden within the combusting ash clouds of life, there is always a point to the eruption to be discovered, so exploding the roof off of life we go. It is time to put the sign up: Gone Mentally Purging!

On Route

WOW, IT IS WINTRY out here today. This should not be a surprise to me considering I heard that it was forty-three times in two minutes on the radio this morning but, like Mark Twain said, "Thank God for the weather as if it were not for the weather humans would have nothing to talk about." This was paraphrased a little.

Of course, being so immersed in my morning, my brain did what it automatically and often does; that is, it deleted information it saw as unnecessary. But sometimes I wonder about how it does this. Do our brains use algorithms—like those used by Google, Yahoo, and other big Internet search engines—to determine what they think we want to be focusing on? Really, just give me the news guys and don't try to cater information to me. Who do you think you are? If you want to find out more about how these and other Internet sites present information differently to people based on what you have searched in the past, please do so. I will say this much; what you do online is not anonymous, so be careful. So much for privacy rights!

Anyway, back to the Arctic chill I am experiencing. My whole body now seems frozen in time. This is not good! Anyway, I hope the heart beat that motors my life kicks in and fast. I have had trouble in the past with it, so there is reason to be worried. Come on baby, you can do it. I get the news quickly; without a pulse, the factory given but not guaranteed "die-hard battery" is dead. I need a jump and fast.

Luckily, I see Bob galloping up my driveway like he knew I would be needing help this morning.

"Bob," I yelp in a panicky voice.

"You okay there, Jamie?"

"No, I need a jump. Do you have you cables with you?" I gasp as my skin color begins to turn blue?

"Of course, Jamie; I never leave without them," Bob states with purpose.

After hooking up the cables, I am jolted back to life—but just for a second. I need some more help here. The cold is unrelenting.

Bob tries again, "Clear!" And this time, success.

"Thanks," I mutter a few seconds later as I get strapped in for my ride to hell.

Bob states "you're welcome."

And that is that; I am on my way.

From the "death machine," as I have always done, I imagine myself using my overcharged security blanket to call work to let whoever wants to know that I am running late but on route. This is my normal custom. With one hand on the wheel and even less of an eye on the road, I use the better half of my inadequate body to concentrate on dialing work's number. It is now nine fifteen in the morning; time is flying by but still at only one second at a time. It is funny how that works out the same way every time. Excuse me, please.

"Hello. Thanks for calling…"

"Listen! Tell Heather that I am on my way and everything is okay."

"Hold on! Get going man! Come on! Hurry up! Yeah, great! Merge into traffic doing thirty-five instead of fifty-five; real safe driving there, sir. Can't you see we have an emergency here?"

There are so many *Cracker Jacks Box* certified drivers out here it makes me crazy and want to play the game, *Grand Theft Auto*. However, if I did play that game here and now, I would be designated as having "road rage" and who wants that? This is not a good condition to be labeled as having in our society, so for now, I will just pretend that I do not have that mental state where people get angry while driving because some drivers are fucking idiots. However, concurrently, I will continue to scream and yell at other motorists like a lunatic on eight pounds of crack cocaine because

I am an ignorant fool—and perhaps have road rage. Let the labels and generalizations reign over my lost identity.

Anyway, as I pass Mr. Bonehead, I present the guy with the notorious, "Thumbs up Award." I would have given the old man the finger but I know that is not a nice thing to do; my mother told me so. I may not be perfect, but I do know my manners. Anyway, bestowing upon someone the "Thumbs up Award" means, "Great job you moron" so all is right with the world. Hey, it is not what you know it is what you can prove, right?

Anyhow, back to my call. Hello? Hello? How rude! She hung up. Oh well, it is onward then; three cylinders and all pistons firing ahead! As I try to move forward, though, I can tell something is not quite right. I cannot tell you what the problem is now as I actually do not know, but whatever; mentally onward we go in the meantime.

THE COFFEE SHOP

SINCE I AM LATE for work, I decide to stop for coffee at, "There is No Amount People Won't Pay for Coffee," better known to us druids as Starbucks. My visits to the holy shrine of mental tree sloths are mostly uneventful but there was this one time that sticks out in my mind. I walked toward the green sign on the door like some kind of flying bug being drawn to the darkness on the other side of the light. Just in front of me was the figure of a not-so-young woman.

Why a green sign, I wondered? Coffee is not green-but money is. Is this a coincidence? Having to pay if you want the syrup of life—like seven bucks for a cup of java—makes one wonder? Also, having the word "bucks" in the store name makes me think twice as well.

At any rate, I am happy with that pun, when you think about coffee, we don't even need the stuff but all over the world coffee has become a huge part of our private and even social lives. Drive down any main road in the USA and there must be at least seventy-three coffee shops or places to get coffee in. I guess drinking a coffee and socializing is better than going to a bar, getting sloshed, and picking up a man who you thought was a women but I digress-make mine a large.

Now, is that a "tall" or a "grande" these days? Why the new usage of words for sizes? Small, medium and large worked quite well I thought. "Grande" does sound better than "large," as it feels more pleasing and royal, but is that bigger than a tall? For sure there is a reason for this change, and it had everything to do with it being better for business I bet.

Is coffee even better for us than alcohol? I am sure it is, but

10

does something being better on a relative level mean it is good for us? I will look into this idea as we move along.

Anyway, I need my coffee so forward march-left, left; left, left... Yes, we are walking around in circles here.

Come to think about it, a study done many years ago stated that there was some compound in coffee that actually helped people to ward off some forms of cancer. This is cool, as many like to drink coffee. But what do the other chemicals do for you? Before I finish typing this book, out I am sure I will read some other study that will tell me. Sigh!

I read somewhere that people with type A blood should drink coffee, as it helps to thin the blood and prevent clots and people with this type of blood are prone to clots. I also have read coffee can cause serious health problems. Conflicting data-what a shock. There is nothing worse than the old "maybe doctrine"-it may be okay but maybe not. No shit Hemlock!

"Are you coming tonight?"

"Maybe, I will."

Well, of course, maybe. Listen; don't tell me something unless the information is conclusive. Take a side already. Is the answer yes or no? Sorry, I got stood up last night.

This just in; a new study claims that drinking coffee can cause strokes. Stay tuned for more news from the "experts" as information becomes available! Oh, as an aside, according to that article I just read, having sex can also cause strokes so be careful while fornicating, people. I guess to cut down on the odds of getting a stroke you should not drink coffee and drive.

Anyway, as I was about to enter "Big Bucks," on that memorable visit, the woman in front of me, who, as I said, was not as young as she used to be-meaning she was ancient-was kind enough to hold the lavish green door open for me. I used this once common, courteous gesture to position myself ahead of her in what could have best been described as a lineup of bipolar disorder patients waiting to buy some lithium carbonate (meds that they take). Now, because I am ultrasensitive, I will clarify that I am not making fun of people with any problem. I love freedom of speech.

Most people I know and see in our world are trying to navigate themselves through life's dark and worrying passageways, which they are taught leads to freedom and happiness, while mentally blindfolded, depressed, strung and stressed out, all the while simultaneously and terrifyingly wide awake—enough to hear the internal screams for help in fact. This is the result of our socialization. Of course, what can people do? They are within the corridors of life and have no way of getting out. What a way to have to live your one and only existence. But this is the world our brains live in, accepting of this truth or not. We think we know things about the world, but being taught something is real or true does not make it so. It is time to question everything. Nothing is off limits. Whatever we are doing now is not working, so desperate times call for desperate measures.

This disease we call socialization starts at the core—the beginning of life—and slowly, over time, filters into and around every aspect of our lives until the brain is fried and we are at our wits end. I know we need to feed the monster inside but not to be conscious of or even question how our own thinking has been hijacked is the greatest magic trick ever attempted and voluntarily achieved. We bipedal mammals like to think we know so much, but without realizing it are really more like one of Pavlov's dogs begging for the bones we have covertly been told to crave than free people, as we like to think we are. Hold that thought; I smell coffee. Ouch! Clap on; CLAP ON! No light in this corridor, I surmise.

You can call me mean or an opportunist but I knew that if I hadn't snaked in front of "Toumai," I would have waited forever for her to order and then even longer, if humanly possible, for the ancient forest dweller to count her pennies with her arthritic fingers. No thanks! I did not want to wait for her to carve a picture of what she wanted into the counter, so in first I went. (Do I even need to be qualifying this with you? This is freedom—justifying my every move that may seem bad in the eyes of some? Even if many, why care?) More about this social dilemma later because, for now, I really need to focus on my story and getting my fucking coffee as habits—especially addictive ones—usually overpower reason.

12

I recall that I was pathetically so anxious to fulfill my morning needs, partly because I had to wait in line for a whole twenty-two seconds and, of course, I really needed my coffee. To my dismay, however, during this call to Eden, I realized that the price of a coffee had gone up—yet again. I was at the breaking point that one morning.

"Hi Amelia, what is going on with these coffee prices," I bellowed like a regal king sitting atop his loyal and royal pig?

"Frost in Clumbina a while back hurt the coffee beans so the prices went up," came back the less than enthusiastic and intelligent reply.

"Clumbina? That's in Africa, right," I said arrogantly.

"What? No, it is near Equator."

"Screw me," I laughed out. I think she meant to say Ecuador but…

"Pardon," she asked?

Never mind, Amelia Airhead, as I rolled my eyes. It seemed like the tenth time there had been frost in Columbia that freaking year! How many seasons do they have down there? I wondered rhetorically. And how does frost in one part of the world affect the coffee beans in another area? Super frost! Look out everyone! One thing I am sure of, though, is the rise in prices across the board had nothing to do with the fact that coffee beans are one the largest traded commodities in the world. Yes, that was sarcasm.

I did consider asking the certified coffee assistant why all of the prices had gone up again, but somehow I just knew the seventeen-year-old, slightly plump, pimpled, and gum chomping girl whose knowledge of geography rivaled only that of my cat Babo would have had no real answer for me—like I needed one anyway. Sometimes, it is just fun to vent.

Before we come back to the now and order some coffee, you may be wondering why I called my cat, Babo. It is a strange name to be sure. Well, in Korean, Babo means silly or stupid. My cat is pretty whacked-out; hence, Babo.

I am now thinking about what kind of coffee to buy—or whether I should buy one at all. I do not want a stroke. Nanoseconds after that crazy thought, I come to my coffee senses and order a physically unneeded but consciously necessary cup of what we should call "human oil." *Dawn of the Dead* meets Mr. Maxwell House—scene one million and action!

After signing the Visa slip and getting a cross look for not tipping on my twenty-eight-dollar shot of molasses, I continue in my quest to becoming a great citizen by getting into my overpriced, underperforming, oil-guzzling, environmentally raping "marvel of technology" in order to get to my underpaying and unrewarding societal duty—my dead-end-career job. My livelihood—meaning, coincidentally I am sure, my job—is the reason I am here on this one small and insignificant planet, or so it seems. I do supposedly have sixteen other hours in the day with which I can do as I please, but I need eight hours of sleep (I actually get six). My work day is never actually eight hours, and then there is the getting ready time, the commuting time, and the never-ending errands to run; so by my estimations, I have about four minutes of every day to myself. This is my downtime, during which I realize how inadequate I am. Wonderful!

Almost In Hell

ON THE SUBJECT OF cars, albeit on an indirect avenue, don't you think it is odd that we feel as if throwing "garbage" such as cups and papers onto the ground is bad for the environment, yet, in the same breath but a different sentence, we seem to have very little problem polluting our world by clear-cutting forests in order to lay down concrete so we can drive around in our sports utility vehicles—which can drive off the road anyway? If decimating our environment—the air, forests, oceans, and now even space—in the name of progress of course, is not considered polluting our world or even frowned upon, then how is pitching the byproducts of the timber and so on onto that very same ground bad?

This is not a book looking into environmental issues or problems but when we see oil spills, landslides caused by deforestation, smog that blinds cities from the most sophisticated satellite cameras, and on and on we go, it is hard for me to figure out why it is up to us little people to recycle and refrain from "polluting." When the environmental mess we see today was caused by the big corporations that have already made their zillions, packed up, and left town why look for that Big Foot-like garbage can that is impossible to find? Oh yes, because we have been told it is the right thing to do. By whom I would like to know. Isn't guilt powerful?

Regarding companies that pollute like Lindsay eight-ball goes to jail-all the time, you may think charging them millions or even billions of dollars for mismanaging the environment is great. But when they have made "zillions," how appropriate are those fines? This is even more curious when you consider many of the companies have left the area rendered useless for anything sustainable for the locals. The tar sands in Alberta, Canada, are a perfect example of land degradation in progress. As for now, I need to get us to work.

Before we continue, you may have the impression that I am a little cynical or jaded, but really I am not. I only appear to be this way when no one else is around. Socially, I am as happy as a killer whale in a swimming pool. So where was I? Dr. Pill? Dr. Pill, come in please. No one is answering?

It is now nine thirty, but it feels more like two in the morning to me—not that this time really has a feeling, but you know what I mean. I pull into the parking lot at work thinking what good time I made. I actually would prefer to leave home a little later on a daily basis because, this way, I'd happily get to miss the worst of the morning rush hour traffic; but my boss says I should be on time like most others. I did ask the den master if it would be okay to present a few less "Thumbs up Awards" on my African Safari-like drive into the labor camp for the poor, but she said no; it is nine or say good-bye. I hate this black and white crap as who cares if I come in a little later but what can I do, rules are rules? Teamwork, there seems to be nothing like it—If you are on the inside looking out that is.

Yes, you little agitator you, I could find another job I guess, but I have been here for so long and I know all of my "duties" well, so quitting is not a great option for me—or so I think. I also don't want to start over and have to deal with the politics of being new and then slowly, again, trying to acquire the bones of slavery-seniority—not that this flaccid achievement does a great deal of good for people these days, but you, I know, get my drift. I am also not sure I could ever find another job that pays as well as this one. I have a lifestyle I am used to, and I don't want to lose that. I have worked hard for what I have. Sure, the things or "creature comforts" I possess are really not making me any happier, but not having my toys would make my life less pleasurable to be, sure so what can I do? Is there an *I* in team? Can I say *I* anymore than I just have? Man my writing sucks! I guess I could try to gain this skill as well, but I am just so busy with...

On the flip side of this equation, how does Jamie really know Jamie could not get something even better than what Jamie has now? Jamie never really tries anything new. Jamie tried broccoli in his pasta once and did not like it, so Jamie gave up on trying new fads or crazes. Jamie keeps things the way they are because Jamie thinks Jamie feels safe, but look at him; Jamie is dead inside. This is an interesting avenue of thought, but the moment passes without Jamie realizing the consequences attached to him making the conscious decision to settle for merely what Jamie thinks Jamie has. See what happens when I try something new. Sigh!

When I think of the "game" we call life, the phrase "short-term pain for long-term gain" comes to mind often. But that gives me a headache. School the first twenty-five years of life and then work for another forty; when is the short part? I would like to get the "pain" out of that equation, but I am just an ordinary Jamie dealing with everyday problems like many others. So what can I do other than go with what I know? If I had more time, I could look into this, but alas, I am at work now. So in through the doors of the parking lot of life I go! Pass the Philips-head as the X on my skull marks the spot where I am about to get screwed royally!

How Are You

I ENTER WORK AS edgy as a gazelle that is being chased by whatever they get chased by because my work place makes me uncomfortable. Not being a specialist on this breed of antelopes, I am just assuming they get apprehensive regarding this scenario, as it is hard to believe that, as cute as they are prancing around like a transient who just found a dime, they love the idea of being eaten if they take one wrong step or make one poor decision. My point is that I feel the same way; my mind thinks that every choice I make is of the utmost importance and that one bad move will be the end for me. I am the gazelle.

Of course, I could stop being late, and the gazelle can only ever be a gazelle but … Luckily, I guess, feeling like the soon-to-be mauled and eaten, four-legged herbivore is normal for me so, all is good. As an aside, it is a fact that businesses in the Western world lose more money every year due to sick days that are caused by stress than any other way, so I guess assuming I am just an unknown number that is part of some grotesque whole is okay. Ignorance is my salvation—here in hell, anyway.

Oh look, a three-legged frog. Frogs are great indicators of pollution in the environment and to the overall health of the natural surroundings. Hmmm—I guess things are not up to snub or are "legging" a little behind around here.

"Hi, Jamie; how are you?" Pete asks the most irritating question known to all humankind?

"I'm okay," I say back halfheartedly.

I really am not okay but the illusion we call caffeine is working now, so things are looking up. I wish I could wake up feeling like this all of the time but oh well…Hold on, is this even coffee? What is going in here? As I work the case, Pete interrupts my thinking.

I really am not okay, but the illusion we call caffeine is working now, so things are looking up. I wish I could wake up feeling like this all of the time, but oh well ... Hold on, is this even coffee? What is going in here? As I work the case, Pete interrupts my thinking.

"I heard you had a little scare out there today. It looks like you could use some cheering up. Here is a funny story for you," Pete rejoices, like a male accordion player who is playing with his retractable slinky.

"No," I blurt out.

But Pete has already started up.

I really hate that question; "how are you?" I think people, generally speaking, don't really care how others are doing, so why bother even saying that—to be polite? Perhaps, but is this really what being polite is all about in our world these days—verbal hot air? The "how are you" question may be considered a socially polite inquiry to raise among friends and even strangers, but the only thing that empty query does is lead people down a well-trampled, predetermined course of inevitability.

"How are you?"

"I am fine and you?"

"I am good. Nice weather today isn't it?"

Shoot me right now at close range with a bazooka!

With regard to the "how are you" fiasco, if you do not methodically ask the same back, whether you want to, feel like it, or even can, you are considered rude. But this is a mistake. Being rude, as I see it, invariably comes down to one person doing or saying something that some other person thinks is wrong.

"You are being so rude!"

"I am not rude. You are being selfish!"

"Stop being so unreasonable, you jerk!"

"I cannot believe how inconsiderate you are acting; childish, too!"

"You are so ill-mannered," and around and around we go.

It is raining ignorance everywhere all of the time, so call me selfish and save me from such idiotic drivel, please. I will just say thank you and then move on. This usually leaves people even more pissed off, but I am selfish, so I don't care.

In the end, calling people rude is a tool to try and emotionally control them, but what a crazy notion that is, as there are over six billion ways to think what is right and what is wrong. People, throw logic and pretenses out the window when it comes to the idea that others are being rude or selfish. Rather, just try to accept one reality—all of us are sincerely trying to be happy and not sad. I have never met someone who has said to me that his or her goal for that day was to go out and be angry; some act like it, but this was not the day's goal to be sure.

Regardless of what anyone may think, people are under no obligation to execute tasks for others, even though we have been told doing so is considered polite. What makes social norms right or even desirable? The square wheel of social life tries to turn to the use of norms, but that "fact" does not make anything literally true or right—especially when you look around and see only chaos. In fact, I think social norms are evil. They turns great, creative, and hardworking people into anger-oppressing, wine-swigging, ak-47 shooting, ready-to-go-off psychopaths; and these are just the women who were knocked down on the street by some rude bastard not named Jamie who did not move out of their way.

Okay, you are on to me. That is right—I knock people down who think they are too good to move even a little bit. Who the hell are you to think you do not have to move? And why am I the bad guy when you do a concrete face plant? Equality, right! Whether old or young, woman or man, fat or thin, and so on, we are all just people. So, princess, don't think you are too sexy to move your fair share, because you are a dime a dozen. You move a little and so do I is the norm, isn't it? Thinking back, though, I should have said sorry. But the ambulance arrived so quickly, and Grandma's hip didn't seem to be broken so ...

Anyway, I think a little more trust in others by our policy making, power wielding social guardians would be nice, considering we trust everyone we see every day in a way. But I guess we need the rules to hog-tie those who just cannot abide by social norms—you selfish pricks!

Anyway, I am not trying to convince you that it is difficult to reply to "How are you?" All I am trying to say is perhaps, sometimes, I don't want to say anything, so back off. I can choose to not reply back like a robot without being bad or wrong. People seem to think it is, though. But for God's sake Pete (or "Jim" from Star Trek), I am just a mammal!

I think if anything, we should ask something like, "What is good in your life?" when we meet someone. At least then we would be directing the conversation into the open and toward something positive and not sad. I mean, really, do you want to hear someone say, after asking how they were doing something like, "Not so good. I had diarrhea all morning and then threw up what tasted like soured cottage cheese and rotten eggs all afternoon?"

As for those candid replies, most would say that the person should have had their mental filter on, right. How many times have you heard, "Too much info John?" So if we do not want to know how John is really doing, why bother asking?

I also like the idea of saying something like, "I see you." Years ago, a friend of mine whose name is Jason told me about this tribe somewhere in Africa that actually does this. The jungle/tree people in *Avatar* say this to each other as well, so it must be good, right?

Anyway, back to Pete and his story, which I have totally missed. Wow, I am being so rude, right?

Hold on; here comes Bob. He is walking with purpose, so I am assuming he has something to say.

"Pete, Heather is waiting to see Jamie. He has to roll."

"Okay. Sorry! Let's talk and move," Pete unilaterally decides.

Enthralling or what! Anyhow, Heather is my "boss" these days. More about her in a short minute as, once she starts talking, I will tune her out and jabber on about her. As for Bob, I didn't have time to talk about him earlier—or better, I didn't want to because he is a little less exciting than his name. Bob is actually a lot like Pete, I think. The last time we spoke, his topic was some minor league baseball player who broke his leg in a tragic, yet comical—well, comical to me, but let's not split hairs—kite-flying accident. As I recall, Bob spoke about this stranger like he was his brother. Earth calling Bob! Do you copy, Bob? Hellston, we have a problem. Boy, do we ever!

ATHLETES AND ACTORS

PERSONALLY, I LOVE PLAYING many different sports, but chatting about people who are glorified in the media because they revolve around the making of money more than anything else hardly keeps my interest. You may think these people are entertaining us, but the reality is marketers who work on behalf of these games are merely just trying to sell us idiotic sticks of ready-to-be gnawed-on gum—some relief from the chronic mental anguish that we have in some form but push aside in order to appear normal to the masses because society runs on having to be part of some larger group. We are constantly being played, ironically; we are chewed up, spit out, and stuck underneath the idea that we do not matter, until the pleasure curtain opens up and we are needed again. Go team go!

Really, how does anything athletes, sports teams, or even actors do benefit my life? These "stars," who are really just ordinary people who care more about their image than anything else, may "entertain" me because my own life lacks meaning, but that really does not make my life any better. Indulging these money-makers may, in fact, make your life worse, as avoiding a hole in the bottom of your boat is never smart when you are in the middle of the ocean in it. You may not be sinking fast, but if you think watching games is harmless, you are taking on water.

Why do you think it is so easy to be pleasured in our society? Try to answer that. Caesar brought us gladiators, and today, our "fearless leaders" bring us guys who do nothing more than play with balls of different sizes. And we love them for it. How have things changed? Anything that can keep our minds off what the experts have done to fuck up our world is somehow a debt paid in full? Man, we are dumb!

In the end, unless you gamble, it really does not matter who won, does it? I mean, truly, does the playing of sports by complete strangers who are making millions of dollars because you are watching them really make your life better? Are you really an extension of some team? When "your" team dies you go down with the ship, too? I think it is funny how many smart people get angry when "their" team loses. Come on people! What do you think the chances are, you gambling fool, that athletes before a game are saying things like, "If we do not win I think we should give the fans their money back?" All for one and...Nope, I am done with that expression.

What a weird investment it is to be a fan. Some game enthusiasts may feel a little pleasure from game to game and year to year from rooting for their team, but most get heartbreak, as there can only be one winner, right. At the same time, all the teams' players get rich, whether they win or lose. Good deal for one of you to be sure.

As for actors and their exorbitant wages, I think we should pay like a buck or two to see a flick and that movie studios should pay the actors less. Really, some people get paid twenty million dollars to act in one movie? I recently heard that Will Smith asked for fifty million to do another *Independence* movie. Come on! People who are slaving in factories for forty hours or more a week don't make that kind of cash in a lifetime. It is sickening to me that people make that much just to perform. Of course, if I were an actor, I would not complain about making a boatload of money. But I think I would feel guilty about making others pay twenty bucks just to see me work. Imagine starting a business that required others to pay to watch you work. You have skills some do not have and would pay to watch, don't you?

"And then I push start, and the coffee starts brewing. That will be fifty bucks please."

People in the news, who put their pants on one leg at a time like you and I do, are just normal citizens with a skill for which they're overpaid. So start pushing for a rebate on tickets to anything and everything. The way to make this work is too actually to stop going to the movies. If these overcompensated people have any heart they will take less money so you can save some. Good luck, though. Personally, I just watch movies at home, if at all.

I never understand what is happening when players on sports teams go on strike. Listen, Joe Steroid, you guys are just employees like the rest of us. Where do you get off making demands such as you deserve more—especially when that would mean we have to pay more for tickets?

Can you, the reader do this? Can you go in to your boss's office and insist on getting paid more money or you will stop working? You could, but I think you would be told no because of cutbacks or some other lame excuse. Or, if you pushed it, your employer would fire you after they said no and you threatened to go on strike.

Are athletes really special? I do not think so! You penis cups are employees to most of the time rich "white men" like the rest of us. So get over yourself and start running around and chasing balls again for the mere millions you already make you spoiled brats! I want to acknowledge there are owners who are not Caucasian or even men for that matter. At what point can we call something diverse? Anyway, I know when your way of thinking gets attacked, looking for holes in the logic bomb so you can launch a counteroffensive is natural, but not here, thank you.

Of course, I do like that athletes have an option to not work and that they stick up for each other. This is cool. I guess you could see this situation being like a poker game; the first person who blinks loses. And if you can play that card-bravo to you! There is nothing wrong with asking for more money, but being able to keep your job while not working seems odd to me. I guess this is what happens when your job revolves around the making of big time money.

Of course, it is the people who go to watch these sporting events that create the idea players can afford to ask for more.

So while many hate that athletes make so much money, it is the layperson who is responsible. We like to get angry at the way the world is, but if more of us stopped playing the rich man's game, things would have to change, wouldn't they? We peasants could never act like someone who merely plays with balls, and we drive the world forward with our backbreaking work; but such is life at the bottom of the societal food chain.

To sum up, stop buying tickets to everything, people! I am telling myself this as much as you. Games, movies, theme parks, and so on are all pieces of cake that taste good at some particular moment; but pleasure comes and goes, as you know, so do what makes you happy.

Personally, I think that, if you want to glorify anyone in our society, praise and look up to people who work long, grueling hours in factories every day for their whole lives. Without these stars of life, that chair you are sitting on right now would not exist. These people really matter, don't they!

I can't believe Pete is still talking. Do I really need to hear this?

"So this golfer…"

This story must be earth-shattering if he is willing to take time out of both of our lives, right? If Pete could only see outside his bulbous head, he would understand a whole lot more about people. Unfortunately, no one has said anything to him regarding his obtrusive behavior. Does he think he is saving lives or something by telling these long-winded stories? Pete, what are you doing? Leave me alone already!

"And when he fell from the tree with the bees still stinging him, he landed on the golf ball he thought was lost. How ironic is that? The worst part was, he had to take a two-stroke penalty for moving his ball while it was in play, and because of that, he missed the cut. He was subsequently fined by the Golf Association and dropped by his sponsors for not being able to live up to his contractual obligations. I feel so bad for this guy. Could you imagine being that unlucky? But it goes to show you how one bad thing can lead to another if you are not careful. So please take care of yourself is the point, Jamie," Pete mercifully concludes.

Thanks for the life lesson, Pete, and for the natural sleeping pill you just gave me. And with regard to the golfer, it is hard to feel sorry for a guy who is making hundreds of thousands of dollars or more every year playing golf because he broke his leg and was stung by a few hardworking bees. Does that golfer care about me? No, I do not think so. He doesn't know about me, of course, but only because of money and marketing and, well maybe, the fact that I have no real talent that would make people want to know me. Anyway, all I could think was that I hoped the bees were okay.

Man, this day is just getting started, and I am already done. Having a mind that continuously runs mental marathons is hard work.

Heather's Office

A FEW PAGES LATER but really only a couple of feet in fictional distance, I finally arrive to where Heather is at. Thanks Bob! Heather is a forty-five-or-so-year-old divorced woman and mother to two things we call teenagers. She also always seems to be happy, although, perhaps not so much today after she is done with me. Her appearing content, however, is something I don't understand as her job is stressful to be sure, to say she is not attractive is being polite, and at her age she is almost dead. Whatever, I guess. Barely awake, in to see her I go. I wish my appearance and condition was a little better, but too late for hope now.

Once in, I can see that Heather has a nice white coat on today. It is very long—too long for me, actually. I have no clue anymore as to what is happening around me.

Bob disappears from the room, which leaves me to face Goddess Isis all by my lonesome. Here we go.

"Okay, Jamie. Let's get down to it. Here you are again. What ..."

What a fake. I can't stand her. She is always pretending to actually care about me, but I know she is just working for money like everyone else. I do not know her well, as we are not friends, but you know sometimes you just get a feeling about people. I could be wrong about her, but this is how I feel at the moment.

"Last year I mentioned ..."

I am so tired. I can barely keep my eyes open for this.

"Are you okay? Are you listening to me, Jamie?" Heather anxiously asks.

"Sure," I mumble.

"Well last year, I tried to warn you that ..."

28

I really need more sleep, but I like staying up late because it is the only time of the day (night/morning/whatever) that our world seems peaceful to me. I use the word "seems" loosely for those keeping score at home. I really do dislike being mummified within my blankets by eleven and then having to be up by six or seven, just so I can plow my way to work on time. I know I have to do live the routine if I want to be part of society, but why is it up to me to like this situation? I have to be responsible when things are bad but thankful when I am offered or earn something worthy of praise? That kind of sucks! I was born into the world with these farmer's hours, but I never remember asking for it. Sigh! Well, I guess for now, anyway, I should think about where I am and hope I get out of here without too much problem.

"Do you comprehend my apprehension regarding this, Jamie?" Heather finally finishes.

"I don't understand," I reply weakly.

I think for a moment about the shot from the verbal cannon that has just flown over my left brow—what does apprehension mean? I am just kidding. Heather is right about me of course, but I do not have the strength to accept what she has said. I feel lousy, but consciously, I can't think I have a problem when I look around and see a reflection of myself everywhere—and hey, this mirror is broken. I guess my life could be better if I tried to make it so, but it isn't and that is just the way things are right now. That is my life; but I know my time will come. My dream is my fate.

"Thanks for your concern, Heather, but I will be okay." My hollow and Razzie Award-winning reply fizzles out from my broken BB gun.

I do have many of life's viruses, though. For example, I have a mounting mountain of bills that require my attention, I need a bigger television because my friend just got a new one, and my health is an area of concern to be sure. These grand issues are my biggest concerns in my life today. They all seem important to me; the first one deals with my financial health; the second concerns my mental well-being; and the third, my literal, overall health. So what's left? But I will be okay; I always am. I always thought that I would be.

"Okay, Jamie. I will see you later. Bob will help you get settled in today," Heather gently concludes.

As we are finishing up, out of the corner of my eye, I see some peculiar object sitting on the table. It turns out to be a book, but a book like no other I have ever seen before. It looks like it has literally been through a war. I can't make out the whole title from where I am, but part of it reads, *D-Day*. It must be about war. I would say something but I could imagine how that conversation would go.

"Pretty wild-looking book, Heather; I didn't know you had an interest in war—death yes, but not war," I would grossly blurt out.

"Actually, Jamie, that book is about one's own self-awareness and happiness, not war. It is a great book," Heather would state in an assuring manner but, as you probably know, into deaf ears anyway.

D-Day, Heather? Are we supposed to be motivated by death? Sounds pretty stupid to me—no offense," I would say. Then I'd feel I'd gone a bit too far because I am ultrasensitive. In quick retrospect, though, being so tired and partially laid out, I wouldn't really care.

"No worries, Jamie. You are entitled to your opinion, but remember, never judge a book by its cover," she would finish like some kind of motivational speaker or something like that.

Heather would be correct, actually, in that we are all entitled to an opinion and have the right to voice that said view, but in a "democratic" society, ironically, doing so can cost you the life that you know.

All life seems to be getting filtered down some narrow tunnel to the point where, if you do not do what is considered "right" by the moral phantom of scorn, you are considered rude, ignorant, a rebel, and the verbal hits upon your autonomy just keep coming from society's infinite number of conservative judges. This is freedom? I can't say someone is old without having others look down on me? I can't share my thoughts regarding a book without having to justify that thought? God damn man, it is a freaking book.

On a broader scale, I shouldn't disagree with foreign policy because that makes me unpatriotic? This is freedom? Screw it; Iran can pursue nuclear technology, as everyone has that right. There, I said it. What do you think of me now? Am I, at this moment, on the outside looking in? Am I the enemy because I choose to think differently than what I have been told is right? Are you thinking, *How can you say that about Iran?* Most do, so good news, you are probably well liked and one of the group. How is that working out for you, by the way?

The unconscious universal norm today, no thanks to us ordinary people for making it reality, is to do what the rich people say and not as they do. These dolts will be a major focus of my blistering tongue to be sure. Freaking crooks! Of course, if you don't follow their rules, you are not allowed to play in their vertical roulette game, where every rotation ends in chaos. What a choice! Life-my life-is a scam, as it was taken from me the day I was born and replaced with the game *Hungry, Hungry Hippo*. My need to consume knows no bounds.

Seriously, why I believe anything is because I was force fed to. This education was not my choice. We are told we have the freedom to make choices, but this can only happen after the foundation of your life-a million norms, values, and stories of verbal cement-has been poured into you and has turned your brain into concrete. You are now "strong," but it is hard to build upon this foundation, as every way you try to turn, you can't because you feel mentally stuck.

As free humans, we are allowed to think what we want, do what we want, and be whomever we want—but in theory only when talking about "the game." Look at me; I am playing the game the best I can, but I am stressed out, miserable, and pretty much laid out on a gurney, just hoping my time will come. If I could teach you one thing—which would be pretty amazing since I never even take my own advice—it would be this: Change is the biggest part of life. Life requires this fact to be true because, without change, life would cease to exist. The world was not always the way we see it now; nor will it be in the future, so there is still hope. Yes we can! Yes we can! I am not sure what I am hoping for mind you but …

Another day just crawls by. If it was not for intravenous life line injecting the office's liquid of life into my body, I surely would be dead asleep by now instead of just slowly dozing off.

I sit back and think about Iran. How can one believe anything we hear or see on the news these days? All major networks and newspapers have their own agendas so what we hear is what some behind-the-scenes people want us to think and nothing more. I mean, really, can you truly believe beyond a reasonable doubt that Iran poses a problem to the rest of the world? Yeah, Ahozlqxghaomadxzinedfozjad, the "leader" of Iran says some crazy things, but so does Mel Gibson, and people still go see his movies. Well, maybe a little less so now, but you know what I mean. And yes, I understand the scales are a little different regarding the two, but the point is that some idiot saying something ignorant does not make his country a legitimate threat to the world or the cause of all wars. He, the Iran guy, is a twit, but I am just saying there are many of those around and we really do not seem to care about them, so why him? Is anyone ready for a new world war?

Now, if Iran is looking to build nuclear weapons, this would change things, but nothing of that ilk has been proven. I think people need to get evidence or shut up. There is no need for another Iraq-like debacle, is there?

To fan the flames a little, even if they are building nuclear weapons, why can't Iran possess nuclear weapons? Nine countries now posses such weapons; along with Britain, China, France, India, Pakistan, Russia, the United States, and North Korea, Iran's reported archenemy, Israel is among them—although, Israel's having nuclear weapons is unofficial according to every report I have read.

At any rate, Iran is building them for sure and there were weapons of mass destruction in Iraq. Interesting! And to further this argument, think about this; if you think Pakistan is more stable than Iran, then let me simply suggest the following—stop taking acid.

As for Iran and the world community, the country did sign some treaty regarding nuclear power some time ago. But over 50 percent of the people in our country said, "I do" in front of "God" at one time or another but are now divorced; like I said, life means change, so roll with it.

Of course, I have been known to be wrong once in a while. Thus, like the paper cup that states that the coffee is hot, I too shall defer all responsibility by saying I am not responsible for being a moron sometimes; so be careful.

I could be as right as a right angle about all of my opinions thus far, but the real question should be and, in fact, is, how has any of this "great knowledge" helped me so far? Look at me. I have all the answers, but I also have one foot in the grave as we speak. It is one thing to "know" the truth but an entirely different egg to make that work for you in some way, isn't it? I mean, I am neither rich nor happy, so what the hell am I doing?

Normal people like you and I are not much different when born than a clean piece of sheet metal that is getting readied to be molded into something on the factory shop floor. We are first shaped by our parents-and they based the way they shaped us on what they were taught (how they were shaped). Then, we are slowly sculpted further when inserted into the educational system. Come high school most of us are close to becoming a finished product. The only thing left to determine is the detailing. Are you going to be a Lexus or a Lada—do you go to university and actually study a profession or is the transformation project going to be over for you?

Once we're done, regardless of the decisions we have made, we are a completed moneymaking product or tool to be used to make others wealthy and, if we're lucky, make a buck or two for ourselves as well as we try to survive daily for the life we think we know.

It is now ten thirty—tick … tick … tick…What the heck am I going to do for the rest of the day? I am here, so I need to kill time somehow. I am going to need another intravenous line, please. Time to doze off I guess. See you later.

Is this a dream, or has the work day finally ended? Well, I think I will roll with this new mental state and imagine work being done, regardless if it's true or not, and head off to the gym. This is what I usually do once work is done.

Before I go sweat my ass off, though, we will be making a quick pit stop to the home of liquid gold—the gas station. I would write about the cost of gas prices here, but then I would have nothing to complain about later, so for now I shall stay mum like a cadaver on this subject and push on out of here.

Just Like That: At the Gym

SO HERE I AM at the gym, like in life, doing the same old thing; I lift a few weights and then usually embarrass myself by trying to run alongside an elderly woman who leaves me in her treads. I love loping beside older women, though—okay, I'm really walking at a somewhat fast pace—because instead of having sports on the television or something suitable for motivating me to exercise more vigorously, they have on some soap drama. Oh no, Beaux Duke is in another coma—run harder! Isn't it weird how we now consider having a "boob tube" to watch while at the gym normal? Advertisers have you right where they want you—running straight ahead and unable to look around.

Striding back to gym talk, how much fun can working out be? It is not like I am out playing sports or eating delicious food. Read into that as you will. I do like watching guys, though, as they, accidently only, bump into the attractive, little bunnies—and then try to get their digits. It is quite a show for those who have never witnessed this primitive mating dance.

"Ugh! Me muscle big...Too make up for a small penis!" How could anyone resist?

I was even approached once. I was so excited as I recall this one episode from my vast collection of intellectual experiences that I have stored in my long-term memory. On that one glorious day, I was working my muscles that are near the ones that are important for doing things when sitting around when this big muscle guy came over to where I was flailing about like an octopus doing yoga on acid. What a catch I was! Anyway, this guy was so big I swear if I had pricked him with a needle, he would have deflated like an erection after seeing three seconds of a Korean Porno movie or

35

the motion picture *Striptease,* assuming such crap resulted in an erection in the first place.

In the age of "The Internets" why even make a movie like this-for the plot and story line? RIP Hollywood-less.

My experience turned out to be a little more than embarrassing—and not because I was acting like a human octopus. I do not care how I looked to anyone, as I am sure you have noticed. At any rate, the "bull" in pure, primal longhorn steer mating mode and as polished as one, tip-treed over to where I was and then, once beside me while yet still five feet away, leaned over to tell me that the machine I was using was, in fact, his. Checkmate! I felt like such a worm as I slithered off of the machine. Oh well, life moved on, and so did the monthly payments for the membership I never used again.

Talking about my workouts, I would like to be doing different things here—hell, everywhere—but I don't. Why I do the same thing over and over is no mystery, so I continue to choose to run this course and not try or perform anything new. I am a one-trick pony, as some would say. Bravo, Jamie! I think I have what is known as "gamblers fallacy"; that is, I think the odds will eventually change in my favor, even though they cannot. As a result, instead of facing my fears and switching tracks, I am betting that the world around me will change and bring me into the money, so to speak. Well, you can bet on this if you desire, but be careful is all I will say. Yes, some hit it big, and following dreams is smart and commendable; but hoping to get lucky is not really a plan is it?

As for gamblers fallacy, or the Monte Carlo Fallacy as this mental phenomenon is also known, you can flip a coin one hundred times, but the odds are always fifty-fifty it will land on either heads or tails. Some think that, if the coin lands on heads one time, the odds change for the next toss, but they don't—especially when you use a two-headed coin like mine seems to be. I did choose heads once, but the coin went down some sewer drain, and that was the end of that. I can never "catch" a break.

Perhaps I am happy and thinking as I do is normal. Really, how would I know? And for that matter, how could someone else truly explain to me that I was not happy? Feeling is not objective; even though we try to think it is. We can't compare feelings like we do the weight of gold for example. Well, looking at me now, maybe you are not buying this, but really I am very happy—so much so I don't even want to cry now. I have some fool's gold for sale here; anyone buying?

Looking into happiness in a bit more detail, if people are doing the "right" thing-living like they have been socialized to—then don't you think more of us would be happier? The average "score" on a test that somehow can measure levels of happiness is six and a half out of ten. That is terrible. Imagine what your life would be like if this was your average score in school. Good-bye to your university or your post secondary education—if you were even accepted into one or could afford it.

At work you are expected to give 100 percent effort, but when it comes to being happy, 65 percent is acceptable? Everything we do in life is supposed to lead us to greater happiness I thought. I think society needs to raise the bar a little here, as I was never all that happy getting sixty-fives in school. Of course, this would have to mean greater fairness for all, which will not happen, so a "C" subject I shall always be.

THE MYTH OF SELF-ESTEEM

WHILE WE'RE ON THIS psychology kick, think about self-esteem for a minute. "Experts" claim they can compare people's levels of self-esteem simply by having chimps do tests and by making them participate in "controlled" experiments; but do you buy that? At the end of these said tests and using the results from these malignant methods, authority figures in the field of psychology can come to some conclusion concerning your level of self-esteem. But who determines what low or high self-esteem is— Morris Rosenberg, the man with the most "popular" self-esteem gauging test? He gets to say what is good or bad based on ten questions? How can experts logically categorize people as having low or healthy self-esteem based on how these primates see the world and on test scores? These trial results are born from within the confines of an imperfect world, so how could anyone on this planet first, determine where ground zero is as you need a base to start and then, second, make intelligent and conclusive conclusions based on those answers? How could one do a math test and be graded on it if there was no logic to how we used and/or interpreted the numbers in front of us?

We base self-esteem tests on what—comparing people who are successful, act happy, die old, offer different answers to pointed questions, and so on to those who think life stinks? Where is base camp? In the end, people are interpreting results and far too many assumptions are being made in this world, so screw self-esteem and other labels that try to define me and my feelings. You may think I am out of my mind carrying on like this, but that is only because your mind is still stuck in the box. Or I am out of my mind. Let's keep going and find out, shall we?

Here are three simple test questions that are supposed to help determine one's level of self-esteem:

1. I am happy? Agree or disagree.
   Wouldn't the answer have to be based on how people perceive others and how they, then, compare their feelings to what they "think" they have seen? The problem here comes down to a simple question—how can anyone know the real answer to this question if we cannot compare our feelings to what we see? Feelings are not visual, and I can never truly sense what others are feeling; so I may say I am not happy, but what was this answer based on? I could easily just be ignorant. Think about that.

2. I wish I could have more respect for myself? Agree or disagree.
   If I say agree, I must be pretty confident to be able to say that don't you think? But in this test, such an answer shows I have low self-esteem. The same problem rests here as above-we may think we wished for this but shifting focus can change this answer in a heartbeat so the answer really was more situational based and is not terminal. People respect themselves more than they realize.

3. I feel I do not have much to be proud of. Agree or disagree?
   Let's see, I grew up in the ghetto, both my parents are in jail, and I am living on the street with three quarters in my pocket. I would not be happy or think I have much to be proud of, would you? If I had such shitty luck, it would not mean I had low self-esteem; it would mean the circumstances surrounding my life are crap.

The bottom line about these kinds of tests is most people truly love themselves but, when answering questions, focus on the truth that they currently believe. Realize thought that what the brain thinks and what is true can easily be quite different. I think we need to be afraid of terrorists but my friend does not. So who is right here? We do not know the truth about life, so considering this fact, there is no base in which to compare our feelings. The idea of low self- esteem does not exist in every country, you know. Tibetans, for example, have no idea what low self-esteem is. And we shouldn't in our society either, as self-esteem is just a useless label that makes no logical sense.

Having humans make assumptions about others is about as fruitful for society as a whole as a sink hole is in the middle of a city. What good is a person who thinks he or she has low self-esteem or believes he or she is lacking confidence in a society where being productive is vital to the survival of the machine. We are helping no one by labeling others anything other than human and amazing. You may think helping others to become better is a noble crusade, but this is missing the point, and besides that, following this reasoning, would we not then have to help everyone?

Self-help gurus in our world today, who are really just snake oil salesmen or cerebral pedophiles if you will, like to show they can help with improving people's self-esteem. But when we realize that this condition does not exist and all these "gurus" are doing is changing what the person is focusing on, their show is really more of a scam than anything else. Don't think of a dancing pink elephant on top of a house. It is so easy to get people to think about something other than what they already are. In the end, someone with "low self-esteem" is just a person without the education of knowing they are already great.

Of course, in today's self-help world we need to see the "positive," whatever the hell that universal picture looks like, or we are depressed. But screw that; things are what they are sometimes. So, what this means is, if I am feeling down, don't try to pin me in some metaphysical corner and tell me I have some condition that requires attention or, worse, try to cheer me up without booze and babes. Why put a load of verbal labeling diarrhea on top of not feeling great if you do not have to? The idea that we are not allowed to freely think "negatively" without being labeled in our society as something that is less than desirable is a joke.

Summing up, if we continue to base test scores about who we are as people-that are insanely in relation to the world we see every day-we are heading down a road of mental anguish-if we are not there already. Scientists need a new model on which to base their fascination with the question, who am I? We like to think we know the truth about something/everything, but the reality is we know less than we think, if anything at all, to paraphrase Socrates.

Getting back to the idea of happiness, if I'm honest with myself, I must admit that I really do not feel happy or healthy. But happiness, anyway, is just some fictitious ideal, so who cares, right? It is something we grade from one to ten—like a math quiz— which shows that society has turned happiness into something mental, rather than a feeling. It most certainly is, of course, the latter so what the hell!

I would like to feel as happy as a lion in a zoo but I am not. And I used that sarcastic metaphor because, while lions are the king of the jungle, in captivity, they are there for our amusement—kind of like me, a human on top of the food chain but enslaved as well. My time will come, though.

Feelings and being able to communicate them to others makes us a very unique mammal. But every day we become more of a cognitive species, and feelings are becoming less important—or so it appears. It seems more and more every day that most of us are like little marmosets that are chained to a jukebox; we're offered bananas once in a while in order to make us look happy so our master can get paid.

I need to be told what to do and think and be a slave to what I have been taught like the world needs another war. Most people wish for peace, but our fearless governments around the world, which are run by people with money, sure know better, don't they? Globalize that thought. Of course, if I don't sing and dance, I go hungry, so let's go pseudo-happiness spelunking.

Definition time:

Happiness: (1) the endless pursuit of the insane; (2) see gambler's fallacy.

Heather was right; I am landing in hot water more and more these days. Have I reached the end already? Is my forward motion, my quest to wherever I was hoping to end up, already over? I am not old; in fact, I am far from it, so I know that this is no midlife crisis I am experiencing. I am doing everything that I am supposed to be doing—or at least everything I have been taught and told was right. I am self-reliant, although, I do not grow all my own food, drill my own gas, make my own furniture and clothes ... Get the hint? We need so many people in order for our lives to be the way they are. So I say to those self-made people, self-reliant my ass, knucklehead; and screw you to those who have messed my life up on the flip side! I may say this forty-eight times on this little journey of ours by the way. I am now insured—not that I am ensured it will help me, but...

Let me see, what else? I finished university—not that that's any prerequisite to anything. I have a job. I do charity work. And I have a pet. So I must be normal. How could I not be?

Yet, I feel like crying. I feel like a misplaced and malfunctioning piece of scrap metal. So much for my molding process; I must have been made on a Friday.

I decide to cut my workout short and leave the meat market. Today is not my century-like day I guess. I start to cry as I think of my family.

OFF TO THE BOOKSTORE, I THINK

AFTER PULLING MYSELF TOGETHER (why is crying a sign of weakness and not strength, as it takes great courage to show such vulnerability—especially in public?) at least in an acceptable sense, as I imagine I know what others think acceptable behavior is, I promise myself I will make up for leaving the gym early today, tomorrow. If I had a nickel for every time I whispered those infamous words, well, you know, I would be broke. Long live the banking system and what a gem it is. No matter what the banks live on-with or without any money apparently. The people who work on the bottom rungs there may not survive, but the institution and its white-collar crooks surely will.

On the subject of the banking system, I highly encourage you to watch the Michael Moore documentary *Capitalism: A Love Story*. It deals with the seven hundred billion-dollar bailout the banks received and the connection between the White House, the Senate, and Congress and companies like Goldman Sachs. What a bunch of conniving, soul-sucking weasels these Wall Street businesses are. Like I have already stated, these scumbags run the government and not the other way around. It is depressing that people vote for change and expect a lot in return without realizing this fact first. Get educated, people!

Now back to my post-workout activities, if in fact, I was ever at the gym. My mind is still a little foggy right now. Before I can go home and relax privately in fear, I have to make two stops. My first stop will be to the super bookstore that opened up near my home a few years back. The place has every book

43

imaginable—even the national best seller, *Travel Afghanistan: Your Guide around the Landmines and to the Poppy Fields of Dreams.* Amazing! I am going to make a little stopover there—the store, not Afghanistan for the record—because I promised a friend of mine I would pick up a book for her. Don't get me started, though, on all of the problems associated with the paper mill industry because I don't know anything about that, and I would hate to look stupid.

Okay, you talked me into it—cutting down trees is bad! Chop, chop, people; time is money is the slogan for this industry. I should have quit while I was only way behind instead of on the stump I'm on.

Talking about the environment, the new big environmental push being thrust upon us normal people is to stop buying bottled water. This actually makes sense. In order to transport this ever-present necessity into stores around the world, a great deal of pollution is created. And of course there is all that plastic. Did you know that far less than 50 percent of plastic bottles end up recycled? Close the pocketbooks, people, and open up the taps—if you're from a first-world country, that is.

As for bottled water, Americans spent over $21 billion on the stuff in 2009. Is this foolish or what? And I thought buying coffee was nuts. With water, you can just turn on a faucet and get results. It is almost in vogue to be carrying bottled water around. I used to just eat fruit and other water-soluble foods to get my water, but now drowning your system is the cool thing, I guess. Perhaps I am getting old.

Anyway, tap water is actually safer in many ways than bottled water, as it is monitored and regulated all the time. Who knows what is happening on some company floor? Many studies state that water from taps is actually better for us to drink than bottled water. Why? This is possibly true because our bodies crave the natural minerals that are found in regular tap water. Is this why some companies that sell bottled water use just regular, repurified tap water for their bottled water? These companies' water is not pure, ice-cold water from some mountain that we have never heard of before; it's plain, old, yet jazzed up water from some water facility plant, or something like that. Madness!

―――――――――――――――――――――――――――――――――――

There is one main issue to address here before I fail at trying to be funny again, and that is the story of fluoride. I love the idea of tap water but the following needs to be said. Just a couple of paragraphs, I promise.

If you think what you are about to read seems crazy, please go look up the history of fluoride on your own. It will make you sick I almost promise you that. Many years ago, fluoride or calcium fluoride/sodium fluoride-before it became the most famous ingredient in toothpaste and tap water-was a byproduct born on the inside of smoke stacks from the making of atomic bombs, among other abominations, such as the aluminum and fertilizer industries. All this happened on the tax payer's dime, no less, to make a long sentence and even longer story as short as I could. Fluoride is a poison, people. It has been linked to many health hazards such as cancer and osteoporosis, while also being associated with people having lower IQs. You want clean teeth, chew your foods more and watch what you eat and drink.

You might be thinking, if fluoride is so bad, why does the government allow this toxin to be added to tap water and toothpaste? Well, many studies show milk is also bad for us, yet this liquid is still everywhere. Why? Money baby, money! Both fluoride and milk are multibillion- dollar industries. How—in a world where money talks and bullshit is used as fertilizer upon our plush mind fields, and teeth so it would appear—is anyone going to shut that cash cow down? Interestingly, not all countries put fluoride into their water systems. Most European countries do not add fluoride to the drinking water, for example. In North America, it is business first and sweep the questions under the coffins later.

What else is "good for us" that we see and use every day? Meds, almost all meats, junk food, fast food, and many other products we consume have all lead to deaths in our world; yet there it is-everywhere for us to "enjoy." What are we being fed here, people? And why? Has anyone ever died from eating too many vegetables, fruits, or even tofu? I've heard men can grow boobs if they eat too much soy, but I already have some anyway so...And magic mushrooms do not fall into any of these categories, for the record.

Regarding the "truth," we humans are akin to a decaying time capsule that is full of life but buried beneath the ground—we never truly get to see the light. We think we do, but the system is like a runaway freight train that is carrying nothing but blinding toxins. So with our blurred night vision goggles on, let's stay on track, shall we?

Speaking of staying on course, it's my friend's birthday next week, and—in line with what now seems to be the norm—she just told me what she wants. I personally do not like this trend for purchasing gifts, as it makes me feel even more mechanical than I consider I already am; but the sails are set, so going about gift buying in this manner is the method I choose to use—because I have to.

Nevertheless, before the bookstore, I need to pay the bank more money and hit the automated teller machine. Did you know they were invented by IBM and the first one was installed in 1972 in the United Kingdom? That was just a little useless and fun trivia for those who like knowing things. Personally, I thought they were more modern than that.

At the Bank

SO HERE I AM at the extremity of the bank—the bank machine. How nice that it costs me so much cash to get my money out of the electronic paper stool. Let's cut the staff, put machines all over the place, and then charge customers and arm and a leg to use them. This is happening while these very same banks are using my money to make bad investments for which, in the end, I will have to bail them out. Nice! I used to cringe when I saw disgruntled employees putting themselves out of work when their jobs required them to persuade people to go over and use the bank machine. Suicide! There should be a law against self-sabotage while at work, as there is for self-incrimination in court. Here is a job for you; go tell people to use the machine over there or you are fired. Yes, this action will eventually leave your position unnecessary, but at least you have a job for now. As a bonus, we will throw in a nice new job title for you—head of the guillotine. I quit—with my head held high!

I still use tellers every time I can, though, as I like the human interaction. Being forced like cattle to stand side by side with others while not being able to even look in their direction makes me feel uncomfortable—claustrophobic in fact. It is like getting onto an elevator but then feeling you can't say anything because everyone is so quiet. I think I am being emotionally suppressed in our world enough already, so I usually say hi to people when I step into an elevator.

I predict this for us humanoids; as we use machines more and more, we will end up looking like aliens as we see them today in movies. Every day, we have less and less human interaction and more with computers and machines, and a result, different parts of our brain will develop and, thus, turn us into large headed and possibly telepathic, people. They may be aliens now, but that is just us in the future. I just hope we turn out to be from the *ET* family and not those from *Mars Attacks*. This is a sign of the times; I hope to be more like *ET* when we have evolved to this point. That says a great deal about who we are now doesn't it; that or my abnormal ideas are as off as Mt. Kilauea's lid is—often and violently. In my defense, though, I think volcanoes are beautiful, and I think we are more like those little critters in *Mars Attacks* now anyway.

I find it odd that we have to pay a fee to take cash out of a bank machine after regular banking hours, during most of which we are at work, but using the machine at the same time to deposit cash is free. I think if it costs us money when we take out our cash, we should get something when we put it in, like a little bonus or something.

Moving along like long fingernails running down the length of a chalkboard, let's get back to the buying-gifts-on-demand movement. Trying to be positive while the volcano is under pressure and ready to explode, I guess it was acceptable for my friend to advise me on what she desired, as if she had not, I probably would have ended up buying her something she did not fancy. I may have wanted her to have whatever it was I bought her, but that is not what gift giving is all about, so go, gadget robot, go. Hold on, my middle finger will not go up.

I really do not mind that she told me, though, as I am so brain-dead these days I can't even decide for myself what to wear to work, out with friends, or on dates—when I had them. I have to "dress to impress" for my boss, clients, and people who I don't know, so in their eyes I'll look like an ice cube—cool and clean.

And it does not end there. Imagine I am talking to myself for the next little bit. I like this, but this color is not in season. This is nice, but it is not professional-looking enough. This is okay, but my friends say it is too feminine, and that this is too masculine. That is too bold, and this is too cutting edge. This is just plain too old … Yikes! I am so used to people telling me what I have to do that I have lost the ability to make decisions for myself. Well, that is a stretch of the truth and perhaps even the opposite of fact, but why my mind goes there is interesting to say the least. We decide so many things every minute, but we take all those choices for granted, actually.

Moving toward the eruption and to conclude this enthralling conversation about gift buying, tie a little ribbon on that fake present and surprise—you have yourself a donation that may as well have been money, you daft queen. Go buy yourself whatever you desire next time, you selfish and spoiled brat. Who am I, your personal shopper? I want this! Go buy it! Fuck me! Buying a gift should be by personal choice I think—not a chore I have to do lest I become out of favor with the group. But times are changing in our fast-paced world, so call me your mule, and off I go. This is actually part of the gift now; I spend my time on buying you a present because you are too busy to do it. Sigh!

"I am so busy" is the catchphrase of the twenty-first century, isn't it? That and "You're so fired your house is ablaze!" A small embellishment there but symbolically rich I think. Anyway, what a way to shut people out of your lives—saying you are too busy. We are stressed-out to the max, but we are too busy to take a break from the life we know?

In any case, I think this has to be one of the dumbest expressions in the world. It's almost like a competition to people isn't it? People are trying to win an award based on who is the busiest—just like who is kindest, who is the most laid-back, and the list of sports in the "Insecure Olympics" goes on and on. I love listening to people try to one-up each other as to how busy they are or how hip and cool they are. My thinking is, here you go; take your medal and zip it please. You win! It may be gold, but more than likely it will be made of aluminum—the world's cheapest metal.

Personally, though, I would rather spend my time with friends and family and not strangers, but then, that's just me. I once owned my own business and worked feverishly on it, but this was fun for me and something I wanted to do; I didn't feel I had to be a slave or else, which is the choice many employees have to make these days. But even if you are working hard, I find it difficult to believe anyone is really that busy, as a study by the OECD found that Canadians worked on average only eight hours and twenty minutes a day; and this included both paid and unpaid work. Americans were about the same, so I guess my four minutes of free time per day approximation was a little off. What a shock!

I wonder what else I know I am right about that is totally erroneous. What do you think? Have I been on target so far? Or is my logic a little off of center? I will look more into this later. As for now, I do not want to think I could be wrong about anything. You know, I need to mind my self-esteem gingerly because I assume I already failed a test where there were no wrong answers a while back, and one more poor result would make me depressed and crazy. So forward we go.

To finish up shopping for others, I do think this trend of gift buying takes the joy out of shopping—a task I actually like to carry out. But what can I do. And I do realize it's contradictory of me to say I like shopping but also blast people who "waste" their time watching sports, as both activities are really just trivial ways to distract ourselves from our lives. But here, I am executing a task and not just window-shopping. My situation does not follow that oft-followed pattern; want to feel better-go shopping. This is great advice if you want to improve your mood for a moment, but it does not really help, does it? Going out and buying a nice but unnecessary present for yourself and thinking it is going to make you feel bigger and better than ever is no different than thinking eating something when hungry will fill you up forever

Anyhow, how good can shopping be for curing mental issues if you can associate shopaholic with other words like alcoholic, chocoholic, workaholic, and I am sure there are other similar words. Nevertheless, after my eight hour work day ends ten hours later at seven, let's run off to the mall to buy some chocolate filled with alcohol. Help!

How long have we been at the bank? Let's get out of here before that group of twelve-year-olds comes over here and busts a cap in my ass and robs me for the forty bucks I think I just took out. I saw this happen on the news, so now I am afraid of all kids who are out and about. I don't think about the millions of kids who are good or the fact I am more likely to die while driving my car; that pink elephant phenomenon is hard to shake. Anyway, as I drive away, I give them my death stare—as they hop into a minivan driven by someone's mom.

BRAND NAMES
AND THEN THE BOOKSTORE

AFTER HANDING OUT A few "Thumbs-up Awards," with the "Golden Thumb" going to a young kid who barely seemed a day removed from elementary school, I pull into the bookstore parking lot. Luckily, there is an empty spot right in front of me. As I position myself to pull in, I realize that a silver BMW is already occupying the space—along with the one beside it. Since when has someone's own opinion of their car warranted them taking up two parking spots? Sure, it is a nice automobile as far as cars and things go, but it still would crumple up and die like a grape in the sun if some crazed person decided to run into it like a hippo would some idiot who is standing to close to it.

On the subject of "famous name brands," what do you think makes some brands worth more than others that are not as well known? The answer is nothing in a comparative and relative sense, and by this I mean that, while some brands may use more expensive fabric for example, it does not make up for the 5 million percent increase in final retail price over other labels who use materials that may be not quite as good. The cost of making expensive, high-end label clothes is not much different than the cost of making some brand you have never heard of before—they are all made in sweatshops in third-world countries.

This just in; over 500 workers in a Bangladesh sweatshop have been killed by preventable fires over the last five years. Tommy Hilfiger has reportedly offered one million dollars to make the shop safer. This news followed the story about all of the fires. I guess 500 is the magic number.

Getting back to sweatshops, what is going on here? Why are some products so expensive compared to others? And why do people pay for them if they were all made by teenagers making ten cents an hour? Hello, Mister and Misses Sheet Metal; welcome back! If you do not get that, good luck, shopper!

For that matter, why do people spend outrageous amounts of money for things like sunglasses when you can buy pairs for like twenty bucks or less everywhere? I do not know about you, but I wear sunglasses to protect my eyes from ultra violet light and to help when there is a blinding glare. The name on the side does not help me with this, as all sunglasses are required by law to provide ultra violet light protection. So who cares about the name? Why pay for a name? Oh, I see, it goes with your stylish water bottle you are sporting there.

Now, before you spend hundreds of dollars on your next pair, you should know that most brand name sunglasses are made by the same company in Italy. There is a different name on the side and the costs vary, but one factory in Italy makes most high-end sunglasses. When I read about this, I was surprised. Imagine buying a pair of sunglasses for five hundred dollars and then finding out some other brand's sunglasses were made in the exact same shop and retailed for much less. Cheapens the purchase I think. It would be like buying a Porsche then finding out it was made in a Saturn plant, don't you think?

While I am spewing contempt for people's decision making regarding sunglasses, I think it is only fair that I look at watches as well. Seeing every rich person styling and profiling an expensive watch around their chubby, little wrists kills me. You are running the show but are dumb enough to spend thousands on something you can buy for like ten bucks? This shows good judgment? Quit hiding behind things, you insecure twerp. I do not even have a watch; I just ask people for the time if I need it. I hate feeling confined by time.

I could go on and on about items like this, so I will stop here; but why do people spend thousands on pens when they cost pennies and why… IDIOTS!

***

As for the BMW that took two spots, I realize that my inside voice has become the outside one. I, Hardy Drew, have uncovered this transparent web of social disdain by noticing my hair-raising rant has warranted an audience. This untimely display of misunderstood anger is an eye-opener for me, albeit just for long enough for me to try and find another spot that was far away from the amused mob. It was forgotten that quickly, luckily.

Am I that far gone? I can't believe my actions just garnered so much attention. I have to wonder what is next for me; will I end up walking around downtown while pushing a shopping cart and shouting about the end is near? Well, it is 2012 this year and the end may be near so anything is possible I guess. Anyway, regarding my behavior and opinions, looking on the bright side…

***

I do give the owner of the BMW credit for buying a silver colored car, as scratches do not show up as well on silver as they do on black—but dents are another story. Why would anyone buy a car that was black, other than for the clean and cool look of course? Black is hotter; dirt shows up on it much more easily; and, as I have already mentioned, scratches are as noticeable as a movie star's inflated cock piece. Or, I guess, it is possible that actors are just happy with their jobs?

On to the next topic like paint gets dropped onto paper by a baby—with no skill or refinement at all. As for the infatuation with penis size is another thing I don't get. The size of a man's penis is simply a matter of biology, as is the size of a woman's breasts. Guys, get a grip—if you can. Sorry, I couldn't help but give you a small little poke there. That does not read well does it?

***

Finally, I find another parking spot just up ahead so in for the kill I go—or, at least there was a spot. That guy snaked in there pretty well. What goes around comes around, so the saying goes;

although, would something not have to come around if it goes around? This is kind of stating the obvious; it's like saying what goes down goes down. But at the same time, I can't just say "what goes around" and expect people to get it, can I? Very strange and confusing but only because a lady with big boobs just walked by and rendered my brain useless.

Since I have this newfound time—lucky you—I would like to quickly point out something that is quite apt here. Why do people drive around parking lots looking for that one great spot, when chances are you could just park a little farther away and saunter over to where you want to go quicker than trying to hit the "jackpot?" I hope it is not because people are that lazy. That would be sad. The time it takes for you to find a spot to park your car that is in close proximity to the store you want to visit hardly makes up for the driving around, wasting time, and almost killing those of us who are walking through the parking lot.

All of a sudden a Helen Keller-like moment almost jolts me awake similar to a mosquito sometimes does at night when buzzing about my ear. Well, maybe I am exaggerating here a little, but I was somewhat enlightened if that counts. Anyway, is it possible this is why people would rather park close to where they are going—they have kids and are afraid of the walk? I guess this idea has potential to be true. People do wait forever to take an elevator up a floor or two or just stand there and let the escalator take them up or down, though, so perhaps laziness has to be a part of this discussion as well. That will have to wait, though, as I see a space for which to park in.

I pull in between two banged-up heaps of modern technology that even Mr. Metal could not use to make a quick and easy billion and then hail a cab to get me through the parking lot and to the bookstore. Wow, I am lazy.

Anyway, as I play *Frogger* on my way towards the bookstore, I come to realize that it is every person for him or herself out here, which is sad. Everyone is in such a rush these days, it appears that they have no time for anyone or anything—well, except for, of course, the mental slave driver they are answering to and, perhaps, "their" team.

As for the day in the life of the lot lizard, it is starting to appear clearer that the parking-lots-are-dangerous idea is quite real. I have almost been hit five times already, and I haven't even taken three steps yet. If I had children, would I want to walk through this moving minefield with them? Maybe not; and since my answer is only a maybe, the glove did not fit, so you must acquit. How could I possibly know for sure that people desire to park in the vicinity of the store they want to go to because they feel it is dangerous to walk through a parking lot and not because they are indolent?

Life works like this in almost every situation as well. Making assumptions is easy, but how often are they right?

You may have some assumptions about me now, but by the end of this book, you may be eating those mental images—if you understand why I have shared with you what I have. Am I mean? Am I ignorant? Am I foolish? Remember, I said earlier that there is a method to my madness, so I encourage you to reserve all opinions about me until the end.

In the Bookstore

I ENTER THE BOOKSTORE with my don't-bother-me blinders on and head straight for the health and fitness section. As I am walking in and around the displays that have nothing to do with books, I see that stupid *D-Day* burn and die book about happiness. The book appears cool, but strangely, I judge this interesting-looking tome by its cover and classify it as dumb. What else am I supposed to do—peek into everything that may be interesting? I am too busy for such freedoms, and besides, I am on a mission here. So forward we go in this tunnel we call my life.

Luckily, I guess, the book I am supposed to buy is right in front of me. *The Super Ultimate How-to Book about Losing Weight and Keeping it Off: If You Don't Have the Money for Liposuction*—hmmm, catchy! Why she wants this book is outside of my realm of understanding. What makes one health book better than the other? Most are written by "experts" or quote studies that have been scientifically executed yet, somehow, they all differ so much? Why do people keep writing these kinds of books? I'll take obvious answers for two hundred please Alex. If you guessed "What is to make money" congratulations, you have just won some self-esteem that will last ten seconds. If you got the answer wrong and thought the answer was, "What is to actually help others," I will give you that one on a technicality. Now go tell people about this book will you, so I can help them out to—and appease my inner most desire to own a Mercedes Benz two-door coup that looks so cool it would make me feel better about myself every time I drove it because my sunglasses are worth only ten dollars.

As for "diet books," don't we already know why we are or

are not healthy? I mean, really, I am a little overweight because I don't know cake is bad for me and veggies are good? Come on, people! If you truly need to buy a diet book, please at least try to avoid books being written by "stars," as those who entertain this avenue of literary thought (and their publishers) are shamefully just attempting to use their name to make themselves more money. These people get their info from the "experts" or other, already published books, just like everyone else.

Don't be duped into thinking you are getting a collection of profound, never to be seen or read knowledge when you buy a diet book from someone who is in good shape and has been on television for one reason or another. People who participate or work in the fields of acting or sports make a lot of money when they attach their name to some brand, but this does not make what they are selling better than other brands or worth the price of admission. How many times have people thought some "famous person" was so noble, only to find out he or she had many problems, ironically, just like most of us? What a shock! Buy what you need and screw items promoted by pseudo-societal dignitaries and "experts."

Anyway, to finish up on diet books, one thing you should pay attention to if you are going to buy a diet book is who funded the studies if there are any. Show me a book touting the advantages of eating meat where there is a study done by the soy industry admitting as much, then you have found truth; but for the most part, some meat-related industry would be the most likely backer for such a study-and result.

Although, that Robbins guy from the Baskin Robbins (BR) family has written some pretty decent books. This may seem hypocritical for me to say but considering he turned down inheriting BR because he believes dairy is bad for you, I will not question his integrity here. In other news, a couple of reality-show rejects should disappear before they get mistaken for goslings and shot.

Definition time:

Integrity: a character trait sold to the highest bidder in today's world.

Do you emphasize the word *expert* now in your mind, whether or not it appears with quotation marks surrounding it? My bet is that you do. Imagine that—seeing something so simple as quotation marks has become part of your repeated behavior, even when they are not there. You may think this is nothing to think about, but remember, even a small spark can bring down a whole forest. What are you thinking now and why? Be mindful of what you are thinking, as your brain is your compass.

This just in, Paris Hilton, the Kadarshian's and the Palin's are getting rich off of my target audience because my reader's lives lack meaning! Make them go get jobs people and stop reading and watching their lame shows!

"Experts" are going to continue to publish test results that misrepresent truth n the name of the almighty dollar, as scumbags will do what scumbags do. Pawns like you and I, however, need to be smarter, so we can smell our way through the crap. This is actually the bottom line of life—the last and only line. If you cannot stand up against what makes you ill, mentally and physically, too bad for you. Harsh, but you don't have to believe what you have just read, right? Get it?

It's not just the meat and dairy industries who feed us (pun intended) this misinformation. These industries are so regulated and subsidized, it's no wonder most people think meat and dairy are good for us. We are shoveled this "truth" about meat and dairy from a young age, so what else are we going to think? I am not sure whether or not eating dairy or meat is healthy, but most definitely believe it is. More about this meaty affair as we go along.

Currently, battles are raging within our society regarding whether or not dairy products are good for us, whether alcohol is okay for us in any increment, and whether coffee is beneficial to our health. There are also disagreements on global warming, fluoride—

as I have already pointed out—and anything else the experts and politicians can find to disagree on, which is everything of course. Really, why so many differences? One answer is opposing views keeps people employed; it is that plain and simple, sadly. What a waste of resources—both human and other! Another reason there are so many people spouting the advantages of whatever it is they are trying to make a buck off is exactly that—it makes people filthy rich.

Do you remember a few years back when there was a huge buzz about how drinking one alcoholic beverage, specifically wine, was good for your health? People jumped on the bandwagon like lemmings off a cliff because the news had to be true. People were actually told to drink and be healthy. Wine sales went through the roof—as did other alcohol-saturated drinks. What a great moment this was for the booze industry.

While the lowering of cholesterol is certainly great for those with high cholesterol level, what about those who don't need to lower their cholesterol? So sorry, but this study did not tell you what all of the other chemicals in alcoholic drinks do to your body. I wonder why. Is it because any amount of alcohol in our body is not healthy for us? Is it because mentioning the negative ramifications of alcohol would not be good for business?

Think about it. If I am already unhealthy and have high cholesterol levels, is damaging my liver and kidneys a bit at a time worth lowering my risk of a colossal heart attack? Maybe, but please, pass me more than a Band-Aid for my multiple shotgun wounds. How about exercising hard and eating better to get into shape? Thinking alcohol is in any way good for us is ludicrous. The alcohol industry sure did a good job marketing this great news, didn't they? But this is how our world is—full of half truths, at best, and deceit. Okay, it is now Miller time.

Now, more recent studies have confirmed what I have just said. Seemed like common sense to me, but the rest of the drunks needed the experts to tell them I guess. This is the kind of sleazy trick I think people need to wake up to. Hell, this is what marketers do all day long; they think of ways to make us believe we need some product, even though we clearly do not. They try to appeal to your senses but, coincidentally I am sure, not to your common sense.

Marketers, including politicians and business leaders, are not only telling you half truths; they are also all lying straight to your face. This "integral" aspect of our lives—the converting of our natural, creative brains to sponges that marketers and lobbyists use to wipe us out with—is part of the socialization process, part of the trend that changes us from human to humanoid. Our becoming consumers and users of goods so we can become the socially content but nightmarishly regressed sociopath is all part of the bigger marketing ploy our society needs fed in order to survive. The revolution is coming soon, my friends.

And if you think you are above marketing influences, then why did you buy that sport utility vehicle? SUV's are not gas conscious; chances are you will never go off-roading as only 4 percent of those who own four-wheel drive vehicles engage in such activity; and when all is said and done, they cost more money than you needed to spend. Marketers are paid a great deal of money, not because they do not do their jobs well. We are all victims to their alluring ways of course. The question now, then, is to what point will you allow fiction mongrels dictate what you think and do? It is up to you and no one else to find the best truth you can for yourself in this warped world. But enough said about this and sorry about the rant; I drive a hatchback.

Before I buy my friend's book, I consider buying myself a book—maybe even one that claims can help better my life so I can become more fucking happy because apparently not doing cartwheels and always smiling means I have emotional or personality problems. As a result of my less-than-artistic-and-choreographed parking lot routine, and due to Doctor Cooley's "looking glass self," society has branded me mentally troubled.

Oddly enough to you, perhaps, I have already read many self-help books, but for some reason I don't always apply what I have read. I wonder why that is. I guess they all sucked. All of a sudden

I feel despondent. My feelings are starting to take over. Look over there—a doughnut shop in the bookstore. Wow, everything smells so good I can practically taste one. Can you? With that said—or olfactory tasted—my internal probe to who I am finishes as quickly and as abruptly as a Canadian summer does. Back to being "SAD" in the arms of comfort food that I read somewhere are actually good for people sometimes! (Along with its everyday meaning of feeling sad, "SAD" also stands for "seasonal affective disorder," a condition in people associated with feeling depressed when a season changes.)

After inhaling a few glazed doughnuts, I do decide to head over to the psychology section. Surprised? You should be because there is no way you saw that brunette walk by. I wish I had dressed to impress. Oh well. If she cannot accept me for me, then she should just walk away. Brilliant! Off to the stacks of shame!

I am now standing in front of a ton of books that surely will make others think I am need of some help, and this is making me uncomfortable. What now? Help! Well, I always think I would like to feel healthier than I do, so perhaps I should grab a book. Brilliant, I know. Sadly, however, for me, wanting something is more like a wish than a definite innate need—like a dream that is lost by morning. I know in my heart that doing a little work on me would help to create a rosier picture, but I have no time for this I decide. I have to keep on working hard at the office so I can give myself the chance to "live the life," so reading is out. I will be miserable in the meantime, but since I will be mentally busy, at least I won't have time to think about that. But how long can the pleasurable experiences I indulge in and that I need to make my life tolerable save me from my feelings? Time has run out; that is for sure! Yawn. Mindfully back to sleep I go.

A Criminal Game

SO HERE I AM among this great, I-can-help-you-for-a-small-price pile of pretentious, ego-serving, but well-written and intended crap. Well intended to make money, anyway. As I scope the plethora of books from left to right, I spot only a few books I deem worth my while to even open up. The first hard covered book I see—selling for ten times the price of the paperback that is resting right beside it under a cloak of dust—is a "national best seller," so it must be good, right?

Is the designation "national best seller" based on the number of books that was printed or the number that was sold? Let me check ... Literally, just thirty seconds later, I have found the answer; a book becomes a national best seller based on the number of books sold. See how easy it is to get information? Hint, hint! Be curious, people!

In any case, this process of books being recognized as worthy of a read is very different than the Oscar's, where movies that no one has seen can somehow be the best picture of the year, right? Best picture to whom, I always wonder—some fictitious elite who, for some arrogant reason, knows better than us ignorant morons who pay twenty dollars to see a movie that grosses three hundred million dollars domestically and a billion worldwide but then is somehow not really all that good? You know what I am saying here. Voting for best picture is, like everything else now these days, political in nature. And yes, I agree, George Clooney was robbed of an Oscar for his stunning portrayal of Matt Stevens in, *Return of the Killer Tomatoes Return.*

At any rate, I really wish there were more accountability in our world today. I think someone should be held liable for the way things are; if no one takes responsibility, how can things ever get better? Isn't taking responsibility the theme of many self-help books? When has a company CEO ever said, "Yes, my bonehead decision making—really just me taking care of myself and my buds—is responsible for all of you being out of work, so here is some of your money back"? Or when has anyone said something as simple as, "Yes, we screwed everything up, and we are sorry"?

Not one bonehead from the 2008 economic collapse came forward and apologized; "it was them not us" is all I heard, anyway. Even that one "gentleman," Madoff said he was good and blamed others for being stupid enough to fall for his Ponzi scheme. What a guy! But his wife is moral, isn't she? Now she leaves him—with the emphasis on the now? He ruined so many people's lives, while she lived like a rich diva, but only now—after he has gone off to jail—is she tired of his "bullshit." These were her words. What a *****! With what I have just said I will also say; it is not what you know, it is what you can prove-luckily for me! I could have said "catch," there, right.

In Japan, business and political leaders take responsibility when things go off beam. The influential chaps there will actually go on television and apologize. Translated for you I think they would all say something like, "I am very, very sorry—so very, very sorry. But bugger off you, because I am rich!"

While you are bowing and down there my friend, why don't you kiss my ass! Rich folk are the same the world over.

My point here is superrich people everywhere may confess to making an error in judgment, but in truth, they are simply acknowledging that they got caught so they can continue to raid the bank of immoral actions and easy money. Look into corruption almost anywhere in Africa, in Italy, Thailand, South Korea, The Philippines of course The United States, Canada, China…and see for yourself; people on the top everywhere are crooks. I am so angry with people like this. I want to use their heads as speed bags—like the ones boxers use. I have been knocked over enough by their melons, so hitting what they use to pull their punches seems fair. No one pisses me off more than rich and greedy jerks. They are so smug; but they're not "better," so I guess I should relax.

I think it would be great if people in a social position of power had to be hooked up to a lie detector take a live morality examination when they spoke to us pawns. Obviously, I am talking about politicians here and those in business with connections to them. We elect these people, and they take their position humbly, or so they say. Shouldn't we have the right to know what our employees are really thinking and, more importantly, doing? Let's get the politicians out of politics and other areas of life like the Olympics and make what we see and feel more real. Next topic!

South Korea wins the right to host the Winter Olympics? This is the third major sporting event the country has won in thirty years or so—not including the IAAF, World Track and Field Championships that were held in the city of Daegu in 2011. South Korea has already held the Summer Olympics (1988), The World Cup (2002), and now the country gets to host the Winter Olympics in 2018? How is it that every ten years, South Korea gets to host a major global spectacle? These are pretty amazing odds considering there are over two hundred countries on Earth. South Korea is, as of this writing, making a bid for the World Cup again.

Regarding the Winter Olympics, the tallest mountain in South Korea is barely 1,700 meters (5,000 feet), and short track and figure skating aside, no one in the country really participates in winter sports. If the South Korean hockey team plays Canada or the United States, it will get trounced by forty goals. South Korea is not really a place for winter sports, especially in the south of the country. But what can you do? I guess South Korea earned the bid for the Winter Olympics fair and square—like getting Jeju Island listed as on one of the new Seven Natural Wonders of the World was fair. What a scam that whole process was.

How about the World Cup? Qatar wins the World Cup—

smack me! How many FIFA members are now under investigation for taking bribes—like half of them? Not only is this sad, but what is worse is that we all know this sort of behavior is happening, yet, no changes are ever made to the system. Heck, the FIFA boss was just reelected, even amid the many ongoing investigations into FIFA. What kind of message is this? Lie, take bribes, and cheat whoever you want to, but you still think we can't question your integrity? Where are our leaders in all of this? Oh, live by the sword and die by the sword, right. Thumbs-up to you, buddy! Oh, and you are so fucking fired your house is on fire. What, you have fourteen houses? Doh!

Anyway, I think that, not only would this test checking for ethical irregularities make for a better and, thus, fairer world, it would make it quite a happier one—for us foot soldiers, anyway. Those who are bigheaded enough to think they can pull the blinds over our eyes may not do as well, but then would we really want these people in the positions they are in anyway if this were the case? Forget them and the system.

Wouldn't it be great if our "leaders" spoke like we know they do all of the time? Let's face it; we know politicians talk trash behind closed doors or when the microphone "accidently" catches them doing so, so why shouldn't they speak honestly when they address us? Why do they think they need to appear polished? This growth upon our common sense needs to be removed. These people are not immortals. They are our employees. And unless we demand that they act more truthfully, the tumor that rests uncomfortably upon our once-rational minds will continue to grow like a third testicle on animals living near Chernobyl.

Just once, I would like to see a real person get elected and not some polished, virtue-spouting, idea-dead robot. Is this too much to ask for? "If you vote me in, I will pillage the coffers my first two years and invest in Club Med. And then, for the next two, I will pretend like I am doing well by you by supporting some bills that make you think you are gaining a better life. Then after I am reelected, the cycle will continue, and you will realize your life is actually worse than it was." You have earned my vote if you can say anything close to that; at least I would know you are honest about being dishonest.

Definition time:

Lip service: (1) the façade of truth and caring; (2) mental screwing.

THE TRAP

I OPEN UP THE best seller to find the human brain dissected into a hundred different parts—the cerebrum, where my childhood lobotomy took place; the hippocampus, which is where my desire to eat comes from I guess; and the pons, the place where we are converted into one, to name three. Yes, I am just joking here.

Apparently, these parts are exposed in order to help me understand what is going on in my brain when I am not feeling happy. What I am thinking now is I just want to feel better than I currently do. There is no real goal or happiness target here, so feeling better than I do should be easy to accomplish. I want to flip the switch and get results, not study how or why the light works. I want what I want, now! I do not want to spend a lot of time on this or that. And don't worry; if I say *want* one more time I will kick my own ass.

The next book I notice is one that a friend of mine was talking about (before I met you) the other day. Holy crap, Conman, look at the size of it! There must be over five hundred pages here. I am not that motivated to be sure. It is funny, though, that people see a brick of a book and think the pages are too numerous to read, even though, over the course of most of our lives, we will read thousands of pages. So don't be afraid; turn away—the pages, that is, not the opportunity.

Also, there is no pressure to finish anything you do start, so give whatever you want a try. If you don't want to keep going, simply don't! Who says that you can't stop what you have started before you finish it? Would you consider this a waste of your time? Would you feel uncomfortable if you started something and didn't complete it? Don't worry if you experience uneasiness when not finishing something as I think this is sadly just a normal feeling. I believe our upbringings have branded us with the phrase "finish what you have started." Thus, we believe this social doctrine is a truism, rather than just an idea. Think about that when you ponder the following; only another forty years of work to go.

I hope you love what you are doing! If not, a few actions can help you avoid "the trap." Don't put yourself in any position where you get tied down. For example, don't get married too soon. Don't start your career job before you have lived and enjoyed a certain brand of freedom. And don't buy a house unless you are 100 percent sure you want to live there and pay off your mortgage for many more years to come. Don't think something like, *If I need to move, I will just sell the house*; look around—no one is buying. People used to pass away at age fifty many moons ago, so an urgency to get married, get your career job, and settle down as quickly as possible if you wanted to live the "dream" made sense. But look around you; now eighty is almost the average age of death. So what is the rush?

The "need" to fall into the debt snare is much like the "need" to finish what we start. How many of you saw only one of "The Matrix" "Harry Potter" or "Lord of the Ring" movies for example. My bet is that most people who watched the first installment saw all of them. We are so programmed to "need" to own a house that we feel compelled to make that so. This solves nothing, of course, as there is always something else that requires needs to be finished right around the corner from your new home.

Having to work your tail off because you have to pay things off is the snare our socialization steers you toward but never really gets you ready for, and it has to be the worst mistake one can make. Even education falls into this category; having to work for twenty years while remaining flat broke as a result of paying society back for the education that landed you your job, which pays thousands into the tax system and the rest back to banks, stinks of preprogrammed mental bureaucracy.

I believe that trying new things is great, even better than finishing them in some ways because, if you learn to open yourself up to new projects or ideas, opportunities arise. Remaining curious and being open to new experiences is the key to life. We can be talking about meeting your mate, new work possibilities, and anything else for that matter. Isn't opening doors just to see what is on the other side more worthwhile than sitting stuck in one room because you are not finished with something? The more prospects you have, the more likely you are to find the right path for you. This idea is just a matter of simple math, really. Those who are miserable feel stuck, even though they are not. If you try something different, if you walk through a different door, who knows what will happen? So make those boots do some walking. As for me, I am determined to open a new book.

I look over and see that dumb, *D-Day* book, again. Personally, without even reading one page, I think the author of that book should read a few of these self-help books. As I have heard some say, "The people who write self-help books are the ones who need the most help."

After looking like a genius while perusing through the mass of books, my alter ego figures that I could spend twenty five dollars better elsewhere. For example, I need more Cheerios and the extra channels on my television that I never watch but maybe one day will? I head back toward the checkout counter and, after waiting for what seems hours but is literally just a couple of minutes, pay for my friend's book. Then, I leave. Exciting reading or what? Next, we are going to go and listen to grass grow on the radio at my home, so come on!

On the way to where I think my car is, I notice it is now much colder than it was just a short time ago. It feels like I have been in bed, and for some reason, my blanket has fallen to the floor, leaving me open to cooler air. I really dislike winter. Why would anyone ever settle here—a place that can become this cold? They, the early explorers, couldn't have kept exploring and found somewhere more hospitable to settle down? Imbeciles! These adventurers come all the way from across the Atlantic, and then the first land they see— or conquer—they call home? Maybe this brain numbing action of people living where they first settled is where people became genetically molded to staying with a job that they hate—even after enduring twenty years of schooling?

Of course, I am just cranky now because I hate the cold, and I'm projecting that anger outward. I know venting is not very constructive when it comes to obtaining positive results, but this is where I am now, so please try to deal with it and understand. At least you only have to deal with my universal intolerance for a short time. I try to cry, but the tears that were welling up in my eyes froze, so now my eyelids are sealed shut. I look around for someone to piss me off, so I can unleash a barrage of "Thumbs-up Awards" and make myself feel better, but no luck; I can't see. I am so unlucky!

Not feeling beaten up enough, I decide to make my way to what I call the human pinball arena—better known as the grocery store. Really, I just want to go home and sleep in my once-luxurious, secondhand bed, but I have been putting off bouncing around and through the aisles of the supermarket for so long I am starting to look a little less than fat.

After looking for my vehicle for about ten minutes, I spot my little baby. Should I really feel this relieved? All I did was find my heap of when-I-am-in-a-good-mood-I-will-run- properly," piece of junk. I feel like crying again because of this menial revelation, but due to my massive eyelid failure, I am unable to execute this simple task. Apollo 13 had it easy compared to this walking disaster that you see before you. At least the equipment needed to get the mission home worked—after they ripped their capsule apart and got super lucky of course but…Sadly, I won't be making it home I think.

Anyway, I need some time alone. I will pick you up at the grocery store. I am not sure if you understand, but I just wish my life had been better. That is not a typo. Within the contexts of my story, I mentally start to make ice but in real life, merely start to cry.

ASSISTED SUICIDE AND THE GROCERY STORE

SO, AFTER ANOTHER LOVELY parking experience, which I will not share with you because I do not want to, I find myself in a life-and-death struggle with a row of possessed shopping carts. My damn quarter is stuck in the mouth of the beast. Freedom eludes me again. I try frantically to jettison the demons from my four-wheeled convertible by kicking the cart and swearing with as much frustration as I can muster. No luck, though. Maybe I should just go home. There is nothing easier in the present moment than giving up.

Luckily, I guess, a "food transportation vehicle assistant supervisor" has seen my comical cart episode. As a result and as quickly as a cow climbs a tree, he comes over to offer his help.

"What seems to be the problem, cart kicker?" he asks while looking amused.

"Well, for starters here, cart dude, I am freezing cold, and ..."

"The name is Assistant Cart Dude. Your powers are strong, kind of old cart kicker, but you are not a cart walker yet."

"What? What are you talking about, you freak?"

"Unleash your fury. Come to the cart side. I am your daddy, for fifty cents."

"What? Can you get these carts separated or not?"

"Fifty cents please," he states.

"What? Can you get these carts separated or not?"

"Fifty cents please," he states.

The young-looking, but still odd and scary person calmly puts one of the two quarters I handed to him into the second cart and then the second one into the third cart, and just like that, he separates the two with a smirk on his face—and with no problem or stress. Who would have thought that the third cart would have been mine and not the first? Obviously, due to stress from trying to park my car, my creative and problem-solving half of what I loosely call a brain was overwhelmed and, thus, rendered useless. As an aside, I just learned about the hemispheres of the brain when I all-too-quickly poked my nose into that one "unsuitable" book back at the bookstore. The moment for greater enlightenment as usual came and went like my pay-without thought.

As an endnote to this episode, looking back, I realize that the kid used to me be—a person having fun and not worrying about what others thought. He was working a not-so-entertaining job and making of it what he could. Perhaps he is what we would call immature, but so what; he was just messing with me—having a little harmless entertainment—so all good, I think. It was at my expense, but if I am so "insecure" that I cannot handle some snot-dripping, saliva-discharging, and mentally childish kid, then what am I suited to deal with? Anyway, let's head on in and do some shopping before I go beat the kid up.

***

As I enter the thirty-six-aisle checkout Super Mart, I realize my front left wheel is moving erratically. I noticed this, unfortunately, after I ran into the two-story high display of pressurized cola cans. Sorry, everyone! As red-faced as the time I was caught masturbating by my babysitter to what appeared to be a boob on my television's scrambled picture screen, I decide to ditch the cart. I then quickly, and in stealth mode, immerse myself within one of the many rows that is plastered with itemized products that can offer you some pleasure—if purchased before the past due date of course. Packaged foods with expiration dates on them-the dog has died, and Pavlov is now sad.

Anyway, free from the mess and now somewhat alone, all I can think while looking around is, *This place is such a zoo, literally.* Have you ever seen animals get fed at an animal jail? This seems no different, sadly. Of course, no one is tearing meat off of bones in here, but the word *scavenging* sure fits. If we could turn these packs of people into jackals, the scene I am seeing here would be much more apt. Welcome to civilization—the poorer version of course, as rich people have their food delivered.

With regard to food, sort of, I find it strange that we free humans are allowed to kill ourselves slowly by eating junk food and so on but are not allowed, when we are severely ill, to have someone—usually a doctor—*help* us to end our terminal suffering. To be sure, this situation or argument about your life and whom it belongs to has nothing to do with "God," as some, unjustifiably, try to argue. If "God" did create me, surely it was done for a reason other than me dying a slow and painful death before I am judged on whether or not I am good enough to be allowed to go to a "better place." This is a little less logical than someone with no credentials spending thousands of hours writing an amazing book with hopes it will be published.

Anyway, this is part of the master plan? "God" is here telling politicians to block legislation against euthanasia or doctor-assisted suicides, and as a result, your mother has to depart this life in a dreadful manner? I guess this is sort of like us here on Earth, though; we work and are miserable up until a vacation luckily comes our way, and then it is blissful sailing. No disrespect to those who believe we are going to a better place after we die, but I don't think it is reasonable to assume there is some greater arrangement for us when suffering has to be or is an integral part of the plan just before that happens because that is the law. I love the idea of Heaven—who wouldn't? I just don't agree with not being able to die on my own terms. I am free to do with my life as I please or, at least, free from having to do with it what some group of people I did not vote for, better known as a government, say because "God" talked to them and said, "Don't allow assisted suicides."

And how are politicians, who are like you and me in theory but act more like droids from Planet Polish, more related to "God" than each individual whom "God" also created? I think the whole argument regarding euthanasia or assisted suicides is about money—with the Catholic Church and the politicians and business men front and center. The Catholic Church wields so much power in our world it is scary. Try to run for office and get elected on a platform of being atheist and see what happens. You can't seem to get elected unless you thank "God" 666 times a day, so religion and politics really go hand in hand—even though there is supposed to be a division of church and state.

These two societal twins are as inseparable as, let's say, two loser "reality show" people who can't live unless their names are in the media in some way—even if the coverage makes them look pathetic. Of course you might allow yourself to look like an idiot to those who follow crap pop reality television shows if it made you rich, right? What is your price? I would have to be paid a hell of a lot of money before I went on some show whose target viewers are insightfully challenged people without lives of their own and embarrassed myself. But then, that is just me. As an aside, *American Idol, Survivor, the Bachelor* and shows similar to this-meaning crappy-are excluded. I guess that leaves the news channels and their unbiased coverage.

Pharmaceutical Companies and Insurance Companies, whose leaders almost certainly attend "the Church of Heist and Holiday Sadists" because it is the biggest front in which to do business in the world, play a big role when it comes to opposing assisted suicides as well. Why? Simply, no one makes money off of people who opt for assisted suicide instead of heavily medicating themselves for the sake of tolerating the terminal pain. So, for this reason, as well as the "God" doctrine, people in the West mostly frown upon this "barbaric" idea of dying on your own terms. Most of Europe allows assisted suicides, as does the state of Oregon, but that is about it. Way to go, tree huggers!

I understand that most of Europe is also Catholic and what I am saying here seems to contradict my idea that the Catholic Church wields a great deal of power regarding assisted suicides and life in general, but, no offense, the United States is becoming quite radical. The push seems to be coming from the ultraconservative, or as some call them, the ultraconservative, Bible-thumping hacks from the sticks. Whatever they are called, those who live religiously by what the Bible has to say may want to reconsider their position, considering it was written by people who could have not been perfect as who is. And let's face the fact the Catholic Church has changed its position on many things over the years, so nothing is written in stone—figuratively speaking. So while you do not need to be a contortionist, being a little flexible is cool.

And my point here is not that there is no "God" of course. Who am I to say "God" does not exist? I just strongly believe that our lives should not be in the hands of anyone but ourselves. The people who work on behalf of "God" are just that—people, and not divine spirits who are incapable of making mistakes. Remember that, please, when you read what is about to come up. When I talk about the Vatican, I am referring to the people, the society, and culture within. Sometimes facts here on earth are ugly. Get over it thumper!

This just in; New York State, and more recently, Washington State just passed a gay marriage law, so now gay people can legally get married. Times are a changing. What is next?

Another topic we could discuss here with regard to "God" and the law is stem cell research. "God" was also the reason our loyal servants struck down stem cell research, or so they said. To allow this to happen would be to go against creation. All I can think now is that I feel sorry for all of those who are suffering. If "God" is responsible for our lives and created everything, then the *almighty* also created the technology for stem cell research, no? Who loses the most if Alzheimer's and other horrifying diseases such as this could be eliminated? Think about that.

The smallpox virus killed over 60 million people until a vaccine was discovered, and I don't see anyone complaining about the cure. Nor did anyone complain about the cures for the bubonic plague, lack Death, malaria-which I am left to guess was also *God's* creations?

I can't keep track of whether I am coming or going these days? Where is your benefit to my socialization I told led to houses and white picket fences? When all is said and done, for the icing on this nut cake, after you have fed the bowels of businesses your whole life, you then give the rest of your money back to temporarily make your final days or years feel better. But, you can't choose to die without feeling the pain associated with whatever illness you have, no matter how long it takes to kill you? How sick is that? Where is the joy? Cynical, I know, but that is just how I see things.

In addition, just recently news story reported that drugs, antidepressants in particular, may not be as beneficial as first thought. Some 90 percent of studies that were not published stated these drugs did nothing for their patients, whereas about the same percentage of published studies claimed the opposite. More magic from those trying to make a buck. If this is a lie, perhaps my ideas on self-esteem are not that far off. How would one really know when, at every corner, some expert tells us consumers otherwise?

Talking about being cynical, there is a saying regarding cancer, and it goes something like this: "Until there is a cure for cancer that can make as much money as the drugs that are used to merely help prolong someone's life, there will never be a cure." This is just a paraphrased quote, so don't get angry with me for this. I recently just lost two uncles to cancer, so I say this with a deep heart.

Have I become desensitized? Am I too brash or impudent? I don't think so. I am as sensitive as they come but when life angers you at every corner like it does me that feeling or emotion is about as common as a Dodo bird.

GUNS AND MURDER

THAT WE ALLOW MURDERS but not assisted suicide in our society is crazy. What? We don't allow murders in our society, do we? Sure society does. Society consents to people murdering others by offering an array of possible punishments for murder, rather than a consequence that renders such questionable behavior intolerable. Now even the death sentence is cruel and inhumane? This is a form of allowing murder. Follow me is you can.

If, rather than allowing convicted murderers to receive penalties like prison sentences of twenty-five years to life or less, we offered some very slow and painful death—something similar to dying from some form of cancer or heart disease spawned by junk food—I think most people would not commit murder. Take the humane penalty off the table, rather than leaving convicted murderers with any decent or livable options, and fewer people would resort to murder. As is, commit a murder—or twenty—and if you get caught, you have food and a place to live your whole life; this is allowing murder to happen. Tax payers will pick up the tab for all of this to, of course.

And if the punishment society dishes out does not make people refrain from certain actions, then society is, to a degree, allowing those actions to happen. Of course, we live in a civilized society, so we have to give murderers a place to live and three meals a day, and those upstanding citizens who are dying a slow, painful death because of a genetic anomaly—a bed in some hospital room. Nice! Perhaps my route was the long way to go to make that point, but wasn't it good? We need to allow people to decide for themselves how they wish to depart this world. I keep murderers alive with my tax dollars, but I can't pay for my terminally ill, pain ridden grandmother to have her last wish granted of being placed to rest? Something is terribly wrong here.

Of course, on the subject of murders, the gun control debate is quite lively in North America all of the time. The United States Constitution states that people can bear arms, but look around you; it is not 1869 anymore. Do people really need guns to protect themselves from other cowboys or Native Americans—like they ever did anything wrong—these days? Citizens may need AK-47s to protect themselves from the people who have stolen guns from stores or other people, but then that kind of proves my point—guns have become a problem, and perhaps it is time to rethink the laws that allow people to own them so freely. I mean, really, other than for athletes to get caught with them so they look tough and cool, do we really need guns in our homes?

Now, I understand that guns may seem cool to some people, but after another shooting—this time in Ohio where eight people were shot dead—perhaps the body count is high enough now that lawmakers should seriously consider, and not just debate about, changing the Second Amendment? How many dead is enough? I would think the changing of this law would end up like the prohibition of alcohol did and drive everything underground, but I believe that, with regards to guns, society is already there so...

Film maker, Michael Moore, reported in his documentary, *Bowling for Columbine*, that the United States had ten times more gun-related crime incidents than Canada did, but he failed to mention that the States also has ten times as many people. The problem of guns in society is not an American thing; it is a North American dilemma. Of course guns are everywhere but where do we live-in the West-so the focus is there. Oh, and Canadians do not keep their doors unlocked. Canadians thank you, Michael Moore, for sending all American criminals north to check out your hypothesis. Crime went down in the United States so much some communities in New Jersey let their whole police force go on permanent vacation.

To conclude this talk about firearms, I wish people could own guns and nothing bad happened because of that. But sadly, this is not the case is it. When you see on the news elementary school kids bringing their parent's guns to school, I think we have crossed the point where laws are untouchable; but, again, that is just me.

Now, it may come off like I am some kind of "blowhard socialist," but in fact I am not; I am quite conservative and strongly believe in personal responsibility. Actually, learning to take care of yourself is what life is all about, even more so in such an unfair world, ironically. I would highlight that last sentence.

That said, all parties—even fringe ones—have good ideas. The right idea does not solely belong to the party that is in power that day. Leadership that governs based upon one political party's narrow point of view is not leadership in any language; it is a school yard chest-pounding contest gone horribly wrong. Oh, this may shock you, pretty much everyone in the world is a "socialist." The day one law gets passed, by definition, capitalism no longer exists. So how can you vote for a Republican and the "capitalist idea" over the left-wing socialists when there are over one million laws on the books in the USA?

Still meandering around the store and with time to kill I want to look at the English language for a quick second.

LANGUAGE AND
THE CASHIER MOMENT

DO YOU FIND IT strange that, when we go out for dinner, we are not ordering cow but, instead, steak? Why the change? Saying "steak" gets people licking their chops, while mentioning a cow makes you want to tip one over. Would you rather hear, "Let's go eat Rudolph" or "Would you like some venison"? Would you rather eat snail or would you prefer escargot? Perhaps we should call broccoli green brains or something like that. Maybe this would help kids think broccoli is cool to eat. When people see a cow, it hardly makes them hungry, but talk about a barbecued burger, and that view changes.

Why do we call the taking of one's life with the help of a doctor "assisted suicide?" My guess is the use of this word, *suicide*, is not by accident. I think the English expression *assisted suicide* is a disrespectful term. It cheapens a person's life and shows no respect to a person who has chosen this method in which to leave this world. There is nothing funny here to say, my friends. I am pissed at the term not because of whether it's politically correct but because people have used it to drive an agenda. I am not sure about this, but I believe most European Countries call this action euthanasia and we here in the West call it assisted suicide. Some countries spell the word *neighborhood* thusly, while others spell it with a *u* (neighbourhood). But the words *euthanasia* and *assisted suicide* are hardly the same, so I am just wondering why the huge difference?

The language one uses to describe a situation will sway people's beliefs about the situation in one direction or another. For example, I could say that I hit a car or I could say I smashed into one; which would you think was worse? Most people would imagine the accident was worse upon hearing the version using the phrase "smashed into," and in fact, many studies done in the field of Psychology have proven this phenomenon to be true. The words we choose influence others' perceptions in just about any situation. Think about what is going on around you and avoid simply following the aroma of the moment. Remember, I got you to emphasize the word *expert* in your mind by merely using quotations around it.

Not only do words influence us, but so does our vision. A long time ago, while back in university, I remember reading a study that showed that, in an election, people—either consciously or not—would vote for the candidate they saw the most signs for. There is nothing like making educated decisions, right. Politicians play to your emotions and not to your common sense because they have to and it is easy.

You want to hear something else wild? Red has been shown to be the best color to wear if you want to win a sporting event. Why do you think Tiger Woods wears red on Sunday?

At what seems like the eleventh hour but really is only just past nine, I find the last of my four desired items and head, as straight as I can, for the express checkout line. One would need to perform trigonometry to truly find the most efficient way out of here these days.

That said, did you read the report on how the displays in grocery stores are actually set up to "encourage" us pods to buy more items? We are never safe—except while in bed, perhaps; but even then, our minds are hard at work reliving our day in some fantastic way—our fears and anything else our brains want to replay. I try to lounge in bed and not think about anything, but you know how well I do with that. Nothing ever comes easy for us hunters and gatherers—or better, the hunted and congregated.

Anyway, after handing out a few "Thumbs-Up Awards" for exquisite shopping cart handling, I happily reach the front lines. To my consternation, however, the eight items or less line is by far the longest of the thirty-six ranger posts. I would use the self-checkout, but being a people-person, I value every minute spent with others. My decision to use a cashier, has nothing to do with not knowing how to use the self-checkout machine.

Oh, look, moving on as clean as a sheet of ice that is covered in sand, there is Grandma counting her pennies. How wonderful. Oops. Made a mistake, did you? That's right; take your arthritis pills first and then start over. Sigh! How is it possible that these cave people always have so much change when, every time I see one of these Neanderthals, they are trying to unload it? Yes, it could be because they have lived a long life and have collected a lot of change, but that is just too practical of an answer for an action that is so annoying.

Well, since I am here and apparently have time to waste, I may as well bring up another pet peeve of mine-the person with fifteen items in the eight items or less, "express" line. Do they all own BMWs and think they are, for some reason, absolved from having to follow the rules? As I look around the barnyard, I painfully realize that I am the only person with less than eight items—not including the little, five-year-old rocker boy and his two piercings, who is holding what appears to be four or five products for his mother—who in turn has about another ten that I can see. Get me out of here!

Just when I thought things could not be worse, the mood swiftly darkens like an albino monkey in a spray-on tanning salon. The product scanning assistant is a former baseball player I presume, as she really seems to love throwing the food after it is scanned. Scan and throw, scan and throw, scan and throw, and scan and throw—ball four, so it is time to take a walk. Price check … PUNCH ME!

Finally it's my turn to play ball. This should be fun I think; I'm stressed-out that the chances of me exploding are two to one, so get your action now.

"Hi," I say.

"Hello. How are you?" comes the reply as she tosses my brown, organic, whole wheat, twenty dollars-a-loaf bread down the thingy like a natural right-hander who is using her left hand for the first time.

At this point, all I can think about is the nice, pink wad of bubble gum she is gnawing away on. Give me a second ... It's cherry gum that she is smacking with great vigor. Well done—it is now dead! I could not distinguish that aroma right away due to the bad body odor emanating from the man standing next to me, just in case you were wondering. Anyway, how great it is she likes sharing her eight sticks of gum with everyone. Would you like a stick of cud, Miss? How hard is it to chew with your mouth closed? The saliva squishing sound just does not do it for me.

Anyway, finally I say, "Peachy, dandy, swell," and yes, I lingered in line for that brilliant exchange with the annoying gum girl.

That greeting actually conjured a smile out of me, albeit, a brief one, so time well spent in my books. Anyway, I just want to pay the ransom and go home. I do try to pay so I can get the fuck out of Dodge, but I cannot because the store's debit machine is down. AUGH!

This is a fine time to tell me, I think. *An exquisite ending to my day.* Now I have to pay out a brick of cash to those who bet against me keeping my cool. The odds were one to one right...Sigh. *Why was my life so difficult all of the time* The brain asked the question but then shut down when it came to the answer.

The train of life, loaded with stress and disappointment, just keeps on coming on this circular railroad line, and I am always tied to the tracks and cannot move. I want to cry. I hang my spinning head and proceed off to my home, spiritually empty and without having harvested any happiness fruit for my day's normal hardships.

Once home, I throw the final frozen dinner I have into the microwave and clean out the Cheerios from Babo's food and water bowl. I really wish I would have changed a few things in my life a long time ago, but here I am, just trying the best I can. I am holding on, but for how long?

GETTING CLOSER TO SOMETHING

THE HAUNTING DARKNESS OF my mind engulfs my reality, blinding my vision from the truth I do not know but desperately seek to see. Sadly, there is nothing to see here—not even me as I died tragically the day I was born. Even still, I somehow manage to keep on running away from the life I think I know.

I dart from the home of death and further into my twisted mind, the place where solitary confinement is the norm. The weight of the world is on my shoulders—or so I think—so I sprint to try and get away. What should I do? What are my options? It has been said that all you can be acting out at any one time is what you are doing then and there, so I continue to run with this logic.

I peer behind me as another moment of my life is lost ... into nothing but faded memory. The land around me is quiet and barren, like a once-plush forest after a fire. What is going on here? I know I have to run but what from truly remains to be seen.

My mind is racing now like that of a contestant on *Wheel of Fortune*. Am I going to get this riddle right? I need some more vowels—and consonants. Help! Meanwhile, while the game is on the line, I sadly continue to run away from opportunity-from the answers I seek.

I still know my time will come, though. What time that is— the end of time or my big break—remains to be seen, however. But for now, all I can see are the dark clouds of uncertainty that are all around me. I need to break the cycle and get off this path. Is that a light? My time has ...

Beep, beep, beep; SLAM!
Oh yeah! That's much better than awakening to a music

station that overplays hit songs and employs morons who think they are funny and pseudo-news people who are too ugly for TV—and yes, I know this is a run-on sentence to the tenth power now, but I got my message across didn't I, so other than boggling your mind with a few hyperboles, which is an exaggeration in itself, and stringing vocal tantrums together like bad Ben Affleck movies, what is the problem? See, I told you I would keep on making mistakes on purpose. I am no liar. Plus, it is too early in the morning to be concerned about this, especially since I am in the state I am. Who the hell is coherent enough to sequence words together with grammatical perfection at this insane hour, anyway? Even the birds are still doing their morning thing, so give me a "beak" and let me crow for awhile anyway I see fit. I drift back into unconsciousness—back to dreaming, where life is bearable.

I am awake again, and I'm still lying in a canoe shaped coffin for the living. The time is seven thirty in the morning, and it feels like I have not yet slept. But what else is new? I don't want to get up, and I definitely know I don't want to work today. This is not any kind of new revelation but, rather, a stronger feeling than the usual I-hate-work-and-everything-about-it spew.

I am not sure why, but I get the feeling my life is about to be altered soon, which of course is not a bad thing. Change sure does scare me. But what could change? The worst aspect of my life, now, other than my literal existence, is I don't feel I have grown in any way over the years—not including my waistline. My life is worse than another "news" story involving some star who commits a crime but then does no time. It is therapy for the stars and jail for single mothers, who send their kids off to better schools in different neighborhoods because they want what is best for their children.

When it comes to the National Debt, the environment, the relocation of factory jobs, and so on, our fearless leaders on both sides of the aisle say that they feel sorry for the next generation. But then some DA's office goes ahead and charges a women, Tanya

McDowell, with first-degree larceny, which carries a penalty of up to twenty years in jail and a fifteen thousand- dollar fine. All she did was enroll her son in a better school outside that was outside of the neighborhood of where she stayed. When it actually comes down to it, the elite frown upon equality for children because money talks and poor kids have to take a bus. So it is time you elite quit using kids as leverage in debates about the future; we know you don't care about them. The school board president actually said that there has to be penalties for those who steal "their" services. News flash—they do not belong to you, you possessive control freak! Anyway, a good morning to me or what!

As for me, I stopped growing mentally and spiritually so long ago I feel, on my best day, like the grandparent of a recently unearthed mummy. On my nastiest day, forget about it. Well, at least it's summer now—time to go find a kid who will mow my lawn for twenty-five dollars. I remember a day when the price to cut grass was five dollars. My job paid forty-five thousand a year ten years ago, but the salary isn't two hundred and fifty thousand now—what the hell! Weed used to be ten dollars a gram too, but the damn drug dealers are getting to smart. Mine went to Harvard but now works at the local Bargain Barn as an assistant to the assistant manager, who, in fact, has been laid off. Anyway, it is time for my legal medication…there we go.

Something different is filling the usually very stagnant air this summer morning. Yes, the cat litter needs to be changed, but that is not what I'm talking about. My intuition is signaling that something is about to take place, but I do not know what life has in store for me, even, though—judging by the apprehension I am feeling—I know it's not good. Gut checks are too painful to stomach, so playing dumb is the approach I will bring into play. What a shock! I guess we will unearth this great mystery later and see if I am right about my feelings or not. For now, however, it is time to start the morning ritual. It is now eight forty-five. Please excuse me.

I hit the shower faster than I can type, which is still really slow because I really don't care about my job anymore and I type with only two fingers. What is the point? I am not happy with what I am currently doing, so fuck it! Even still, as per usual, after my shower, I get dressed and again realize that my clothes have shrunk. I feed the cat enough food to last a week, and then it is out the door and off to work I go. My life may suck, but at least Babo has real food now. Thanks, Mom. Let's roll.

At "Big-bucks," I buy the usual coffee and leave without even commenting on the 7 percent rise in prices. This time I heard it was due to the rise in demand around the world for dairy products. Give me a break—I take mine black. See you at work.

THE AWAKENING

I FLOAT INTO WORK like a balloon in the breeze, thinking I had made good time-only one middle finger, I mean, "Thumbs up Award," to hand out this morning, I reckon. Did people's driving become that much better over night? My thoughts about this subject are ruthlessly interrupted.

Hi, Jamie. How are you? You okay? Heather is waiting for you, so let's roll," Bob remarks.

Good morning to you to, Dickhead! Are you going to allow me to answer any of these questions, Bob? How are you; let's roll? What the hell! If you are going to inquire about how I am doing, at least permit me some time to reply, I think. I now have to ask permission in order to answer your questions? Sigh!

"I will see you soon, Jamie," Bob states caringly as he takes off.

"Gurgle," is my reply.

We are now back in Heather's office. Although, is it really hers? We are so possessive, aren't we? That is my pen, and this is your car. But when it comes to my life, sorry! When you listen to people, you notice that they really do claim many things to be theirs. Here, take my seat. That is my chair. Why are using my cup? This is my lane! There is no way you can be free when you feel the need to claim everything as your own, as then you are owned. Anyway, here is Heather.

"Hi, Jamie, how are you feeling? I heard you had a tough night," Heather starts off.

"Hey," I jest while not even caring about my disheveled appearance.

Even though my dream may be my fate, an eerie feeling takes possession of my now-dying body as my skin tone passes by pale white—if white is even a color. Here comes the world and I can't stop it. My running will not help me anymore. Here we go.

"This is not easy for me to say, Jamie, but I don't think you are going to make it here," Heather states calmly but in a very serious tone of voice.

I bob and weave as I fight for the life I think I know but never really cared about.

"What? Why? There must be something I can do," I reply noticeably worried. My legs are now crushed. I start to mentally sprint faster towards nowhere. "I am doing everything you said," I blurt out before I am cut off at the waist.

"Jamie, I told you …"

Here Heather goes, trying to make herself seem like she is not the terrible person here and it is my responsibility that I am where I am. Sure, Heather, whatever! I cannot stand the whole "it isn't me" rhetoric. I can't breathe as Heather tries to explain her theory on life and death. Why am I even listening to this, as apparently there is no future for me here? I would get up and go if I could, but I am in no position or condition to budge even an inch right now. Luckily, Bob walks in and breaks the tense moment.

"Bob, help me," I ask with my voice quivering like a crying baby asks for his mom.

The demolition has been completed. I am barely hanging on now. However, I am free to go, so that is what I do. I start to cry but briefly so. I hate saying good-byes and people feeling sorry for me. I will be okay, everyone. Bye! I will see some of you all in the afterlife. I am not sure where I will be, but the options are limited, so I will see some of you later regardless of where I am. If I had a choice, though, I would not necessarily want to go anywhere. Rather, I'd come back to this godforsaken Earth and torture all those who pissed me off over the years. Crap, I am going to hell.

Freedom

ONCE OUT, SURPRISINGLY, I did not feel that my situation was dire; in fact, I did not feel bad at all. I was not feeling great to be sure, but considering what had just happened I kind of felt emancipated. I had not been run over or killed. I'd stopped running, stood up, and looked fear in the eye and won. I had no more worries about a job I hated; stress; moronic bosses; and most importantly, early mornings that did not have happy endings. Have you ever felt like this before?

My brain, for the first time in recent memory, actually could smell the blossoming flowers of life. This is reality, I thought. This is how life is supposed to be feel—happy and without the side of being stressed-out. I should have left that dead-end job a long time ago. Of course I didn't quit because I wanted to keep or continue to receive what I thought was important—seniority; security; and the most vital of resources, money. I needed hard currency to pay for the bills I accumulated when living my brilliant life, so I had to work. I realize, though, the money I made did not really make me happier but, instead, helped divert my attention from what truly is important. I am not sure what really matters or is essential to me actually but, like when buying a toaster and then realizing a better one was on sale and for less money, you have to make your decision work for you. So, I did the right thing—whatever it was I just did.

Regarding money, the more I had the more I spent, probably to "relieve" my stress. Isn't that fucked up? As a result of having the "privilege" of extra capital (ironic use of the word, as a capital is the most important city in most countries) to purchase the creature comforts that made my life easier, I craved and desired more money. I had to try and keep what I had the way I thought I wanted it. And then of course, there were always models of just about everything that needed to be upgraded. What a vicious and unrelenting cycle of stress and unhappiness this caused, for me anyway. It never ends; you need the new iPhone and iPad; the new Samsung flat screen television; a new, upgraded, smaller but faster computer with xyz data ports, the new Windows; and everything else presumably, as all electronics and software products can be upgraded. I think there has been a short circuit somewhere along my line, as this makes no sense to me. Sure, I do not understand technology well, but you know what I mean.

Of course, one could contemplate the following; was it my own thinking that precipitated the life that I led or was it the socialization my brain undertook without my consent that is to blame? Which is responsible for my great misfortune? And when I say great misfortune that is a relative term, given where I was born and considering those unlucky enough to be born in Mali, for example, where over the half of the population makes less than a dollar a day. Let's be realistic here; we are all pretty lucky relative to most others.

As for questioning whether I am responsible for my life or whether the responsibility lies with the liars who told me over and over to go to school, get a job, and then work hard, I would have to say this is a moot point as well.? Bingo—it is moot, and I have been muted. Don't ask questions when the answers will not help you in anyway. Maybe I will ask that mime over there, however.

We can scream all we want, but no one will hear us. It would be nice to hear an explanation as to why some societies seem to be going down the pisser, though. I mean, if things are so right with our world—and yes, world, as life does not merely live in my backyard—why then do most people I know or see around appear to be so miserable and why are others willing to kill themselves for what they believe in? This behavior hardly seems like something any kid growing up, no matter where they were born, would want for his or her lives. Look around and tell me what you see. Perhaps I should just look into my patch of life and do with it what I can. That said, not seeing the big picture kind of led me to where I am now, so which is right? I think I am going to go with my garden for now, as if I can make it flourish, all will be okay in my world I think.

With regards to physically healthy people who kill themselves, is being miserable a case of, you are who you associate with? Self help practitioners preach the following a great deal: "Be careful who you associate with," Maybe there is something to this? Sorry, we went from suicide bombers to just plain-old suicide here.

Surrounding yourself with a circle of friends who are a rung up on the social or ethical ladder on which you are standing may make sense in theory. However, it's a crappy theory. I may want to upgrade my friends, but I was born into an area full of people like me. And therefore, I associate with people like me. What can I do about this? Don't we usually associate with whoever happens to be around us? How can I become friends with someone who went to Harvard when I went to Hamhung University of Education, a great school in North Korea? Does any Queen or Prince hang around with his or her help or even go to the local mall without people protecting them—even when the mall has been closed down for security reasons? Can we even touch these people? Sick freaks! Who the hell do you think you are?

After a quiet moment of feeling uncomfortable, I try to move on but quickly realize that I am still in my mind. Damn! Well, talking about rich people, I hate all "royal" families. You are born into a family and this makes you "royal?" I don't think so! Folks like these are just normal people who were lucky-if you even see them as lucky. If I saw the Queen of England, I would most definitely try to shake her hand, but only because I heard she does not like being touched. Old lady-you were born into this family. You accomplished nothing! Go drink some tea or something and get lost. Now, back to a real life I think one can relate too. No, that was not supposed to be funny.

I was now feeling great; however, my next thought inadvertently got the sphere of fear rolling again. You really need to plant new seeds deeper than the roots of what you know and water them often if they are to outgrow what you have always been thinking. The brain's life wires are strong and fiercely intertwined, to the point where they are almost inseparable—like a person and his or her cup of coffee first thing in the morning. Heck, don't even talk to me until I have had at least two.

Anyway, the thought I had that sent me for a mental tumble was this: *How am I going to pay for everything I already have?* I started to worry, as the embedded seed of fear—the thirty-five-year-old oak tree of all reason—stands strong within the charred forest of thought. I was feeling like a renovated carpet—new but ready to be stomped on again. My moment, my sense of freedom was lost for the second time in my life, but on this occasion forever within the synapses of my socialized mind.

I decide to go to the gym instead of wasting my time sitting here focusing on what was not right with the world-my world. With the help of my wannabe sports car, I wander around aimlessly, not even noticing Guinness phoned offering their congratulations in breaking the thirty-minute record for receiving the most "Thumbs up Awards." As you probably know, however, it was not really a thumb that I saw. People can be so uncivilized. Would you like a crumpet?

As for me, now, I feel like I am out of the computer-generated matrix we call society and in the real world. This may be a reach in terms of my feelings and reality, but that is okay. I do think, however, that, if I am forced to fight my feelings just to try and find "positive" meaning in what I am doing, it's possible that whatever activity I am carrying out may not even be worth my time. We normal humans are so conditioned to believing we must find the silver lining in this fictitious world. In reality, this idea is crazy; it's just another tool the rich use to take advantage of us. Give me what you have and you go find the silver lining, rich guy! No! What a surprise.

Maybe I will write a book about a world where everything people are taught, such as what is good, desirable, important, and so on is turned upside down from the current hypocrisy. The wealthy few are not prosperous, and in fact, there is no money to speak of at all. What would be valued would be honesty, love, and compassion. The twist would be that the switch between the two worlds would happen overnight, so we wake up as the same people but in a life where what is cherished most has changed. Who would have the problems then? Who (if anybody) would have low self-esteem issues, then? Would psychological terms such as low self-esteem even exist? Anyway, this is just an idea that needs more thought, but so far so good, I think. Can you imagine such a world, though? Pretty cool!

The tangent is now over—if we were ever not on one; sadly, my "storybook" life continues. There really is no waking up from this nightmare, so on with the story and away from reality I say.

"POLITICS"

FEELING FREE, IF THIS is even what I am feeling, is truly wonderful. And I don't mean liberated in that I am able to vote for someone who is specifically chosen to represent a political congregation. This is not freedom. Voting is the mirage of freedom. All over the world, the diversion we call politics is a joke. For example, in Canada, over 80 percent of all elected officials come from the wealthiest 20 percent of the population. Although, some bar worker just won a seat in the Canadian House of Commons-a bar employee who dropped out of school and even went to Las Vegas to party while the campaign was on. I am not sure I like this either, but I did say only eighty percent so...

In the United States, it costs hundreds of millions of dollars just to run for office. In recent elections, Ms. Whiteman—or something like that—spent all of her own money. And why? To take a job that would earn her a couple hundred thousand dollars a year? She couldn't help more people by giving the $300 million she spent away to people in need? Her voice needed to be heard in Congress? Sure, her bid for office had nothing to do advancing her own rich needs to ensure the best for her family in the future generations to come or for her ego. Well, she was not elected. So think about the following: Her $300 million divided by roughly the per capita income in the USA, $30,000, would have made about ten thousand people with nothing quite happy. Instead, she lost a lot of money and helped no one. Well done!

Globalize this thought and see the big picture—billions gone and for what exactly? Employees who our taxes pay while they are still making millions from all of their side businesses? On top of this, these select few get nothing done while you are slaving away on the factory floor just so you can make ends meet. Yep, that is government all right. Donate the money you usually give to political parties to charity and get a tax break so you can afford to pay your government employees' salaries. What a screweded up system. There are checks and balances, but really this means the people who get elected keep getting checks and have to work hard on balancing their own books.

It is sad that if you do not possess money, you cannot help others in this way—being an elected official that is.

And why do we call these people "officials?" Do we need referees telling us what we free people should be doing—especially when you consider that we pay them and that we do so regardless of whether our economy is doing well or poorly? If the NHL or NFL ever went under, the referees they employ would be out of a job, but government workers not only get to keep their jobs when there are shutdowns and the like; we have to keep on paying for them. Nice gig!

Last year, Donald Trump wanted to run for office, but what would make him a good leader? Would his success in business translate to success in office? Does business success qualify you to be in charge of an army and social programs? Countries are now being run like businesses, and this is why Trump looked like a viable candidate for either the Republican Party or as an independent. Personally, I am always weary of billionaire business people who want to work for me.

News flash: Trump is out of the running for President, as you probably heard. Looking back, I guess the whole birth certificate thing was too much for him to face. I am talking about the Obama birth certificate fiasco here. Either that or he thought he would automatically be anointed boss and the rest of the people running would be cast like those on *The Apprentice* and have to fight for a seat. Seriously, this goes to show you what is wrong with the world. He didn't even announce that he would run, yet his approval rating was over 20y percent. Then one little thing happens and he drops below 10? People, what are you basing your decisions on? This especially goes for that "Pallid" woman from Alaska. If she gets elected for anything ever again, I am moving to the moon.

The problem with thinking business first is that only the stockholders benefit from this form of policy. It does not help the masses if, let's say GE, does not contribute to the tax system. What makes society go is and always will be the people; we have to buy products, recycle, make charity donations, and on and on we go. And Wal-Mart tellers asking if you want to make some contribution to some charity as you are checking out does not count as a company helping out society. In this case, Wal-Mart takes that money and, yes, it goes to charities—well, to the people who run them anyway—but the corporation actually gets a tax break on that huge donation. So the execs at Wal-Mart are really only helping themselves to a tax reduction. And like I just stated, the money goes to the people who run the charities. Look into the Red Cross if you want an example of corruption at charitable foundations. Everywhere you turn, someone at the top is, pitifully, trying to rape good, honest, and hard working people. It could be government, big business, sports franchises, charities, and the list never stops.

Getting back to Wal-Mart, people are not helping any charity when they give some cashier a few bucks—they are hurting themselves as instead of Wal-Mart paying billions into the system in taxes, they pay next to nothing because this is one way companies avoid paying taxes—making contributions to charities. Do you really think Nike pays Tiger Woods $100 million to use its equipment or to wear a hat? Money is funneled off to his charity organization and both reap the rewards in the form of tax breaks. So as a result of rich folk and companies bending tax rules for personal gain, we normal folk, golly, have to do more heavy lifting to make ends meet. We get those same tax breaks to people if we donate money to a charity directly so if you want to contribute money, do it on your own and get your own tax break.

Getting back to voting and politics, I don't hate politicians, though. I am more upset at people like you and me, who keep on voting for these self-serving individuals. On top of all of my other arguments, when these guys are in office, we pick up their tabs for just about everything they claim as an expense. What a shock it is that these people are not paying for their own parties. Sure, have a coffee or drink on me, I have three bucks left from my pay.

If the taxpayer's money was not wasted like it is today, we would be a lot better off I think. Who disagrees with this? And I am not talking about the money going towards taking care of people here; I am talking about our money going to things we know nothing about—until our trusted elected officials are caught. Disregard politicians and their crooked ways is my thinking. If you want my vote, you are going to have to pay for it. What is good for the skunk is good for the possum, as both have to live. So you can reek of success, and I will lay over for you but only after I get mine, Pepe.

As for politicians and politics in general, I last wasted my time on them/it, when I was back in university. I ended up voting for all of the candidates because I thought if they could put all of their heads together, they might be able to come up with one new idea. This did not work, but at least I tried.

Sadly, the only affair politicians are engaged in now, other than trying to look good to "their people," is making "less viable" candidates seem more incompetent than they are. At the same time, these same ideological transformers try to market old ideas using new words and terms that their campaign handlers think will make their Manchurian Candidate look like the better of the two evils. You are not as smart as you think you are, Le Pew.

Personally, I think the only way to get our government back is to, ironically, not vote. Starting a revolution would be cool too, but that takes too much work and not getting up and off the couch is much easier. Imagine a whole nation not voting—what a message that would be! Politicians, stop wasting my tax dollars or I will stop paying taxes. How about that? Then we would have a real government shutdown, wouldn't we? Who do these people think they are? You can spin your job any way you want, but I am not buying it; nor are millions of others, so smarten up or meet the end of my boot as I am kicking your behind out of the office.

Definition time:

Politicians/hookers: (1) people that offer you lip service; (2) people who screw you; (3) people who, in the end, you pay one way or another; (4) one in the same.

Since we are talking about politics, I want to talk about being politically correct. Wow, where to start? Could any phrase or immortalized ideal be more ridiculous than, "politically correct?" Earlier, I mentioned that a person was old but in today's world of modern thinking—if being told what to say can be considered a modern concept—that exercise in free speech would be considered a politically incorrect thing to say. I must admit that the idea of not making others feel badly is cool in theory, but there are words in our language that fit like a glove in some situations because they say exactly what they mean. To tell someone that he or she is getting fat is considered rude nowadays. So what should someone say? That the person is flat stomach challenged? In Korea, people say that you are fat without a second thought if you are. And why should I be responsible for other people's feelings, especially when our world is teaching us in many ways to take care of ourselves, as the government is not big brother?

I don't think we should make others feel badly about who they are or are perceived to be on purpose, but the "politically correct" revolution has got to go. If someone calls me poor or fat, I know I have a few choices I could make with regard to my actions and feelings. I could get angry and be sensitive, or I could look at myself in the mirror and decide that maybe he or she is right and I should do something to change my situation. In addition, I could think the person is wrong and dismiss what has been said by using a few choice words. Acceptance is important, whether right or wrong, as what we choose to have faith in guides our boats.

Someone saying, "Wow you are great," is the same thing as

him or her saying, "You suck." The two statements are the same thing—just an opinion—so who cares. Why get up for one and down or angry for another. Neither matter. Many of us like to hear good things rather than the not so good. But I would ask you to think why that is. Are you being sold something? Are you naïve? Do you need hollow reassurances? Does it make you feel good inside when you hear something nice about yourself? What happens ten minutes later? Is that feeling gone? What now? Do you have to go please someone again so you can feel worthy? Think about all of this.

As for people who are just being mean, well, sticks and stones can break my bones, but names will never hurt me, right? If negative words don't break us, then how does being politically correct make people happier? Did you do the "quotations" thing there again when you saw the term "politically correct"? Just testing to see if you are paying attention to how easy it is to become a follower.

Anyway, I find it kind of condescending that people feel the need to lie to me because they think I can't handle the truth. Screw you, buddy; give it to me, you "coward." Yes, I am poor, but you are an idiot because you think that somehow I don't know that. See, what is wrong with this, you Muppets reject? I once heard a guy say this to another right after they first met. Soup? I love soup bra! Word bra! All I could think was, quit trying to be so agreeable you little twerp!

To conclude our discussion of "politically correct," do and say as you wish is my philosophy. It may not always work, but it is my life to do with as I please, and I plan on doing just that for as long as I am around. That said, I think that will be only for about for another one hundred pages, so as I try to stretch my paralyzed legs, let's psychologically move on.

In Pieces

ON A SLIGHTLY DIFFERENT topic, I think it is funny in a sad way, so not funny at all, that on this one blot we call a planet, some people feel that they are so much better than other people. What the mind thinks is just that, a thought, and a thought may be as accurate as CIA accounts of the existence of weapons of mass destruction in Iraq, so be careful.

This wonderful human skill, thinking, and how we take in the world are based on where we were born, which, of course, is nothing more than a random happenstance. So being born in place A is no accomplishment. This planet has been so hacked up by those with the power to influence that people seem to be more diverse than they really are. We are one planet in one solar system in an ocean of galaxies. Our planet has seven continents, an ever-changing amount of countries, states, provinces, districts, neighborhoods, classes of people, races, sexes, gender preferences, political parties, and on and on we go. When and where does the madness end? Are we really that different from each other?

With regards to geography, however, invisible mental lines-or in some cases, big barb wired With regard to geography, however, invisible mental lines—or in some cases, big barbed wire fences— can prove beneficial. Knowing you are about to enter North Korea and not South Korea could come in handy. However, in the same breath, when it comes to people, I wish there were less emphasis placed on differences and more on similarities. We are all people first and then what we believe in second at best. I could be some guy from Thompson, Manitoba, Canada, and find the love of my life on the other side of the world in Asia because love can be found anywhere if you take the time to look for it. I think Hallmark is on the phone for me now. Excuse me ...

Wow! Great news! I just won the Publishers Clearing House top prize—I am being evicted! I will have to gone by the end of this book, so let's continue on, shall we?

I said "hacked up," rather than "divided" earlier because humans are so divided by the erroneous divisions that have been created by the hacking that I feel we're more in broken pieces than merely divided. As for the hacking here on Earth, I guess this is still not finished, as Russia just planted a flag on some submerged ice shelf in the Arctic. As of this writing, it is the year 2012, yet, without it being obvious, we really are still just barbarians who wear ties instead of bear fur.

I pull into the gym parking lot feeling bored. That was too dry. Funny how I seem to know so much, yet, look at me now. Anyway, I pull into the gym parking lot feeling almost too calm to exercise; but that feeling changes as abruptly as the Canadian weather does because, as I am pulling into "my" soon-to-be parking spot, a car trying to save a second clipped the back end of my finely tuned and antique automobile. Other than when being "smashed" into by someone else, my car is a piece of rusted-out crap.

However, amazingly, instead of blowing up like a Pinto (too dated?) would in this situation, I remain stoic. Where is my royal pig? I think to myself, *My car is just an object, so who really cares?* Some may consider a scratch to be an imperfection and bothersome— that it makes their oversized gadget we call an automobile less appealing to the naked eye or less valuable. To me, however, a scrape on a car is like a scar on a person—it builds character. I recognize that a car is just as a thing—an object of no real intrinsic value. A car's market value is only what we sleepwalking humans make it worth. As soon as you take an automobile off the lot, it loses like 20 percent of its value, so thinking your car is an investment is bogus. A mobile marvel of technology may be invaluable to you in that it gets you to work and back, which is important because you need money to pay for your car, but that is about it. Cars are tools and nothing more—sort of like a hammer. But you don't worry if your hammer gets dirty, so why care if you get a scratch or two on your car? It seems that very few people today live congruently. But that's okay; it's your maze to figure out. Just like this book.

Either "things" you possess are important to you or they are not, and now to me they are irrelevant; so instead of getting angry, I decide to see this insignificant accident like I do the last four pages, as irrelevant. I make your mind up to settle this harmless little incident without even handing out one verbal "Thumbs-up Award" and move along with my day, as it is going so well. I am so mature! But perhaps it is best we head into the gym quickly, anyway. Infer from that what you will.

At the Gym—Once Again

WOW, WILL YOU LOOK at this place-or better, smell it! I need some sweet-scented nose condoms to protect me from the stench. Anyway, something more important has stirred up one of my other senses—my sight. I seem to be attracting a lot more attention here today. Usually, this sort of interest would render me incapacitated, but today, no. *Did I forget to put my track pants on?* I wonder as I look down?

Nope! What is going on here? Maybe I am emitting an, I-am-a-happening-and-happy-person vibe today because I am in such a good mood. I do feel like I am floating on a cloud now—like the Goodyear Blimp or maybe the Hindenburg.

Let's go pump some iron. Those pink weights look good.

My workout is going great, or at least as grand as a workout can go. This may be due to my switching up my usual routine, but who knows? Why I always did the same thing here, almost day in and day out, is beyond me, as I think I know a great deal about working. But whatever, today is running well, so who cares why? There is nothing like learning, is there? A house-to-house encyclopedia salesperson came to my door once and asked me if I wanted to buy a set, but I thought he was joking.

Anyway, I still warmed up, stretched a little, and then hit the weights before getting to cardio, but today I did my weight training out of the usual order. I am a wild and crazy person. I am my own best and worst fan—how pathetic is that? Or is it? Some may think cheering yourself on is being arrogant or verges on narcissism to the tenth power, but why is that? You need to love yourself first, so the theory of love and life goes; so why not show that love to yourself, Adonis? And if, in theory or logic, you cannot change others around you or make them do what you want, it makes sense to be your own best fan, doesn't it? If you are not willing to take the job, then why would anyone want it? It is hard to support someone who hates him or herself, isn't it? I would suggest not being too cocky, though.

There is a difference between being cocky and being confident; and to the smart-ass; it's not just the spelling that's different. Being confident is a way of life, and acting cocky or arrogant is just a way for some to try and cover up their imperfections. This course of action, though, is as transparent as the Vatican's connection to organized crime and not worth your time, so don't worry about people who do this. Did I just hang myself? Am I self-publishing now?

As for the Vatican, it may very well be one of the most corrupt countries in the world thanks to its national bank, The Institute for Works of Religion. Have you heard of it? It was started by the Nazis, the Italian fascists, and the Mafia in 1941. The institution does not keep records of its transactions, and all files are destroyed every ten years. The bank has branches all over the world, including in tax-safe havens such as the Cayman Islands and the Turk and Caicos Islands. Donations to the Catholic Church are tax-free gifts as well. I person who received free donuts at a baseball game in the United States had to pay taxes on them because it was a gift. Think about it!

Italian banker, Roberto Calvi's murder has still not been solved. And of course, let's not get into the $2.5 billion dollars the bank has paid out because of all the child sexual abuse cases involving priests all over the world. The list of questionable behaviors does not stop there either. But remember, the actions are by people and this is what you need to keep in mind regarding everything in life; we are all just people. We provide a lot of rope to people in our world because really, we are naive, but this does not make what is going on in the darkness of day and right in front of our blind eyes okay. Let's continue on shall we.

The Vatican also helped to smuggle out Nazi war criminals via the "ratlines" after World War II. This should not be a surprise, as the Nazis helped set up the country's bank, but did you know that people like Franz Stangl, Gustav Wagner, Walter Rauff, and Joseph Mengele, the Angel of Death, all escaped Germany via these appropriately named ratlines. Pretty sick, isn't it? These people were responsible for the murders of millions of people, yet the holiest place on Earth helped set them free and, in some cases, to keep on torturing other humans.

The Colonia Dignidad was a German-run "village" set up in Chile and possibly run by a former Nazi murderer. The reputation of this place is scary, to say the least. Stories of torture and murder have emanated from its bowels like Jack the Ripper stories from the back alleyways in London. Heck, even the current pope was a member of the Hitler Youth Group. Of course, back then, he had no choice but to join as all teenage boys in Germany had to, but this is still interesting I think.

Look up all of these facts for yourself if you don't believe me! It is all public information. The Vatican and its bank are not as pure as one would hope, sadly. And again, "God" has nothing to do with this country. One can make the connection if he or she chooses to not see the truth about this place, but let's get serious here—people run the Vatican, and like any other country, it is fallible to the mistakes and greed of humans.

This just in: The Vatican is getting pounded by accusations of fraud and corruption from all directions. The pope is also not doing well with some asking him to step down. Yep, that is one hell of a country there. I think that many people in positions of power start off hoping to be able to do the right thing, but sadly, the world is not run in a way that facilitates such a desire behind the doors. And you become who you associate with. Everyone is allowed privacy of course, like when going to the bathroom or having sex, but when it comes to business and agreements between countries, what happens behind closed doors should be open to the public. We get to catch the leaders of countries at the lecterns sucking each other's genitals after the fact, but that is about it. Behind closed doors is where the truth lays, and in public is where we get laid out and screwed.

Anyway, the Vatican and its financial institution are quite the bank and country. Try to stay in business in the USA or Canada with the Vatican's track record if you dare. How the Vatican's bank does stay in business of course is not much of a mystery, is it? "God" is off topic and cannot be prosecuted, so what can anyone do? That there are rules for this bank and a different set of rules for all others is crazy. But the world functions on a dual set of rules—the haves versus everyone else.

Do you hate me now? Has what I said struck a "I hate you chord" within you? Good if it has. It is about time someone challenged you! You can kill the messenger, but turning away from the truth and toward "righteousness" will not capture that hidden anger you are feeling and take it away. Anger needs to be questioned in order for it not to return again, not silenced under a cloak of beliefs. I just shared with you some facts about this great "moral" bank. Look them up if you don't believe me. I encourage you to research everything you think you believe from now on.

But just getting angry leads us to another label—intolerance—one of the worst in my books. Not accepting others based on what you assume is right and what you think others are doing wrong because of what they believe is a scary way to live your life. Guess what? Every person in the world has some different views than you. We are like snowflakes—the same yet still all different in a way.

There is one thing all countries seem to have in common, however; it appears that the entire developed world is addicted to plastic surgery. Do you know which country leads in the most procedures? South Korea. Having lived there, I can confirm that. Every second princess has had at least one thing changed. The most popular procedures are eye or nose jobs. Most people in South Korea prefer to have round eyes, opposed to the ones they have now, and a higher nose for some reason. They love their country but not their look, apparently. Crazy!

Anyway, getting back on topic before a hit gets put out on me for speaking ill of the Vatican and saying we actually know nothing at all, if you do become irritated with cocky people with crabs that act like verbal pinchers upon your nerves, instead of scratching, feel compassion for them. If one feels the need to boast, he or she must be nurturing a good deal of pain inside, and that is a hard way to live. I AM THE BEST, in a humble sort of way. Win! I am so positive now!

As for exercising properly—really getting back on topic now,—I am no expert in this field. I do know a few things, albeit at the novice level. Just remember, nothing is rocket science other than rocket science, so don't make your workouts more difficult than you need them to be. Do your weight training first and then do your cardio. Yes, this is the way it is done and not the other way around. You can take that to the bank. Everything else may bounce, but ...

And please remember, if you are just starting an exercise routine, take it easy. Don't do too much too quickly, as your body won't be ready for the shock. If you do over-train, your body will become fatigued to the point where, ironically, you won't even be able to get up the energy to go to the gym. So why do this to yourself? Getting and being in shape is not a sprint to the finish; it's a way of life. So take your time and be careful. Let me say that again; being healthy is a way of life, not a short sprint. Investing in your health is just that— an investment for a better life. So don't be like so many others who try too hard and then burn out. Put another way, don't be a health club's favorite type of member—the one that never shows up. I used to run a health club, and sorry, we needed this to happen.

If you think that last statement was cynical, think about this; do you really believe any gym could handle all their sheep showing up every day? Just for fun, the next time you're in a health club, ask how many flock members they have. Notice how proud the person is when they tell you the cushy number. Go count the number of treadmills, for example, the facility has, and then do the math. Gyms want your money first, and if you are good-looking, maybe a little more than that from a few staff members after hours. Discouraging, I know, but many gyms are just meat markets and, of course, businesses trying to make money like any other. The latter was my focus of course. Anyway, it is time to move on. I would love to talk more about being healthy, but I have so much to share before my time has come to an end here on Earth, so laterally I stay and forward we go.

Post Workout

THIS WAS THE BEST workout in recent memory for me. Maybe I should mix things up more, like I do my logic—often and with no rhyme or reason. Giving your body a curve ball is good for your muscles. Scrambling up your life, like a lotto ball getting to drop in some weekly draw, can help keep the mundane a little more exciting. Taking a different way to work once in a while or changing meat loaf night to Wednesdays from Tuesdays may not knock you out, but it may just help keep you from acting on those thoughts about bungee jumping from your office window without the elastic thingamajig.

That said, if my life consisted of having to eat meat loaf and thinking taking a different line of attack to work would make a difference I would choose the bungee jumping. That's just me, though. I really only mentioned changing things up because I read in a book somewhere that doing so was a good idea. But personally, I would truly try to change the meaning of my existence if this— hoping taking a different way to work would somehow give me a spark—is what my life had come down to. Oh look, I have never seen that 7-Eleven before. I wonder if they have Big Gulps? Sure!

It's time to move on to the next extreme thought, which will be way off the mark because society has become so twisted that logic has outlived its relevancy in day-to-day life-assuming it ever had any ever. Nevertheless, these days you just have to deal with things the best you can and move on. So let's go before we lose our jobs or get spanked, audited, fined, yelled at, embarrassed, ridiculed, persecuted, and on and on down the razor blade-riddled, self-esteem fun slide we go. Once at the bottom, well that's it—you're done.

Moving along, I decide to kill two birds with one stone by ... No, WAIT! What a terrible idiom. Killing birds is not good. I shall, instead, maximize my time by accomplishing two things at once. How lovely does that sound? Holy freak, I've become that Tony Roma motivational guy. You know who I'm talking about—that guy with the nice teeth who is always on the television. Maybe I should become a self-help guru. What do you think? I would be different; that's for sure.

Anyway, back to reality we must go; although, I kind of like it here in dreamland, where there is no judge and no jury. But of course, we cannot stay here; we have to do the mature thing when we find ourselves flirting with fantastic dreams or desires. It's very peculiar that being mature means being responsible and not having as much fun as we did when we were younger; but to what I ask you? You would think that, considering we are here once on this fat and wobbly little planet, we would realize that having fun, being silly, and enjoying our lives should be right up there on the importance ladder with things like working at least forty hours a week and doing everything else we have been told is proper for an adult to be doing. Sure, I need a forty-hour work week like I need another version of Windows. Sigh, back to reality before my computer crashes.

Since I am in no rush, I think, for the first time in months, I will go and do some real grocery shopping—this after I get some calories into me. Yes, I said calories, even though new studies claim we are motorized by little charges in our cells rather than by calories. However, I'm currently focusing on the point that we don't need protein after a workout, so forward we go.

Normal people—not those who are seriously bodybuilding but those who are just trying to feel better than a dead slug—need calories after exercising and not just a pile of protein. We need glucose to keep us going. If you do not eat anything after a workout and the storage of glucose in your body is low post exercising, you may feel faint because, guess what, the body's greatest consumer of glucose is your brain. Fructose, as an aside, is the naturally occurring sugar that is found in foods that our bodies convert into glucose.

As for glucose, around 70 percent of what you intake gets eaten up by your nimble brain. Without glucose, your brain will close up shop, and in today's world, who can afford having that happen? When thinking hard, your brain burns over one calorie a minute. Have you ever felt tired after an intense conversation with some idiot who did not understand how wrong they were? Guess why! Why? Well, since you asked, your brain had to work incredibly hard and thus had to use a great deal of the body's stored glucose, so you felt whipped. You say at this point of extreme fatigue that you are mentally drained, but the reality is there just isn't fuel left in your tank. If you want a great workout, do a crossword puzzle that is way too hard. Let's move on as I am getting tired.

I really could go on and on about this topic, but I will not. Just remember this; excess protein intake has been linked, but the link has not officially been confirmed, to many health problems, including osteoporosis and cancer. I said linked to and pointed out that the link hasn't been confirmed because, in today's world, the truth is hard to prove, as I have shown in some way I think. Some may truly think that meat and milk, both proteins in the ever-changing food group pyramid, are good for us. But even if they were not, we are a pleasure-seeking crowd, so if it tastes good, in it goes, right.

Of course, if flesh and liquids from other animals were not good for us, the meat and dairy industries would spend millions to convince us otherwise, wouldn't they? What would you do if you were going to lose a billion-dollar industry to some bean movement? And milk is a protein, so while some think drinking milk is essential to good health, there does seem to be a correlation between drinking milk and higher rates of osteoporosis. There are many reasons for this, but I want to point out one apparent fact you may not have thought of. Asian countries consume the least milk and the fewest cases of osteoporosis, while the West consumes the most of the former and has the highest number of cases of the latter? Why do you think that is the case? And of course, I said apparent because, well, I think that is obvious by now.

We require the amino acids that make up a human protein and

not cow or animal protein, as it is. We break those proteins apart, and our bodies make human protein from the amino acids that we have just eaten or have stored naturally in our bodies. A human protein requires twenty of these little dynamos, but we can get those almost everywhere. Eating rice and beans forms a complete human protein for example. Eating meat for protein is as ridiculous as is drinking alcohol to improve your health. I mean, let's be serious; people eat meat because it tastes good. I have never gone for dinner with someone who stated that they needed to gobble down a pile of glutamic acid, tyrosine, valine (all amino acids found in protein), and so on for his or her health. A person may say he or she wants some lean meat for his or her health, but then what does that say about meat? I love the taste of meat, but the reality is it may not be as healthy as we would like it to be. That's all I'm saying here.

Getting back to milking cows, please do not just take my word for it; go look this amazing, run of the milk fact up-just like everything else that I have "uddered" as well. However, remember to always look at both sides of any story before making a decision on what you think is true or right. Reading one opinion and throwing your support at it is as smart as thinking you're Superman and hurling yourself from a rooftop after successfully jumping off the first step in front of your house. That first step is a start, perhaps, but your brain accepting you know something because you have read it somewhere is not really any different from believing you already knew something before you started to read. So where does that leave you—other than in the hospital getting treated for schizophrenia? Our thinking makes life more difficult, I think. I now have a headache.

Don't just flip-flop from team to team because it's the convenient or hip thing to do. Be a scientist all the time. Conduct studies to determine what makes sense and allow what you see to speak to you. Then morph what you learn and see with what you think you now. Living via the social media or doing things because this star said do "this" or voting for a politician because he or she said "that" is not the best way to live life. Trying new fads is okay, as you never know what may help you unless you try, but spouting wildly about this or that being the best is as annoying as the notion that an erupting volcano knows what it's doing. Yes, I see the irony.

Back to exercise, I know working out makes me feel great and does the body good, but before I ended up where I am now, very unhealthy, I just did not have the motivation to be healthy. I really let myself go. There is no looking back, ever again—other than to learn from where I have been. Sadly, for me, every time I tried to perform this maneuver in the past I kept running into walls.

Is that Heather? No, it is not. Okay, I will continue on with my story now.

PRAYING, NATURE AND OTHER THINGS

WHAT A GREAT DAY this is turning out to be—even with the light rain. I have always thought it strange when people allow their moods to change based on something they have no control over, such as the weather. Is allowing yourself to think that your feelings are at the mercy of Mother Nature—an entity you have no control over—the best plan with which to live your life? It's sunny so I'm happy? It's raining so my knees are sore and I'm miserable? Both situations are as sad as those two sentences.

Mother Nature is the best. Sunny or raining, a nice compliment or criticism, in the end you are the same person, so who cares? Personally, I love all aspects of nature, including volcanoes, tornadoes, tsunamis, and even typhoons. It is sad that people lose their homes or, worse, are killed by these types of natural events, but that does not make them less amazing.

This brings me to another pet peeve of mine, which I'm cringing about as I type. Why do people say things like, "I pray for those who lost their loved ones," after some accident or natural disaster? How does this help? This is what being kind in our world has come to? The person lost his wife, and you are going to pray for him? If praying helped, these sorts of tragic events would never happen. So how does prayer help post disaster? I really hate it when people say this. I do not hate the people, though. Hating a person and hating his or her actions are two very different things. Doing something unintelligent does not mean that you are stupid. We all make mistakes, so no harm, no foul. Mirror, mirror on the wall…

Last year, a violent storm roared through the southern United States killing about three hundred people in the process, which of course is heartbreaking. But hearing people say that they are praying for the people after the fact makes me question where people's minds are. You are going to pray they recover well? They just lost everything—Holy Moses! I am not saying praying is bad or wrong, although, my writing thus far may seem to point to me saying so. What I am saying is that I believe it is insensitive to say anything about prayers right after some disaster, personal or otherwise.

If I had just lost my wife or kids, you may as well tell me to fuck off, as nothing would compute with my brain anyway. I would be too gone, and I would most definitely not want to listen to people telling me they will pray for me. Prayers do not help bring people back or rebuild homes; elbow grease usually does, though. Spending time with and showing love to your child or throwing money at him or her is a choice we all make. This is similar with people who sit and listen to you and help you rebuild your home after a tragedy and others who say they will pray for you. One course of action takes effort, the other, not so much. I think the transparent illusion of morality and our inability to comment on this freely because political correctness has us bound, gagged, and lying on the floor in a dark mental closet is making more problems than it is solving. But that is just me.

On the flip side of praying for people, there are those who, instead, trash-talk others in the event of a massive natural disaster. For example, in South Korea, one priest said the earthquake and corresponding tsunami that devastated Japan in 2011 happened because the Japanese primarily pray to a rock (Buddha) and not "God." What? Come on! I am sure these comments had nothing to do with the South Korean's rabid hatred for the Japanese because of what Japanese did to their country (they took it over and colonized it) back in the early to mid-1900s. Again, having lived in South Korea for many years, I can tell you that many South Koreans really dislike Japan as a whole (the United States as well). People, governments make problems, not the people. Don't hate a country or its people because their leaders are morons.

I would like to ask the South Korean priest in question how he explains why the Southern USA was torn apart by savage tornadoes and many people there were killed. People residing in the United States south are not religious? This thought is like saying oceans hold no water. This one con man who calls himself a priest later stated that his amice was draped over him a little too tightly, so a lack of blood was reaching his brain. Oh, you poor thing; here, let me help with you with that lariat.

I think people should show some respect and keep religion out of situations like this, as one person's beliefs may be different from another's. People who want to help should just donate money, clothing, and nonperishable items, as praying and knocking those with different beliefs than your own does nothing but show poor judgment. Of course, if you are within a group who thinks alike this would be okay, but how would you know this?

This praying gimmick is just more lip service in my mind. "I thank 'God' that I didn't die and pray for all of those who lost family members?" Sorry, but I do not get it. Even worse are those who thank "God" when they win a game or something. Hello, what about the majority of those who lost—too bad? This is the plan of "God?" "God" makes Tebow go? His belief that this is true may help motivate him, but when looking at his stats, saying "God" helped him is something I am sure "God" is not too proud of. I hope he does well, but let's keep things real, "God" has nothing to do with who wins or loses games.

Do you believe that "God" has no confidence in anyone to ever make his or her own decision or obtain his or her own results? I am sorry to say it, but that—that I have no control over my life—doesn't sound good to me. What kind of "God" has no faith in people yet requires us to have faith in him/her/whatever 100 percent?

And I am not talking determinism here. The philosophy behind determinism is we can do only what we are doing at that time, as everything is based on past experience. A ball on a pool table cannot move unless another ball hits it first. The history of the one ball affects the actions of the other.

And again, this is not to say there is no "God," but when it comes to people, not everyone thinks the same. So I think keeping dialogue in a neutral area is best. Ask if you can help or wish someone well, but offering to pray for a person is a little too in-your-face, and it is borderline ignorant in my books. Does an atheist or a follower of some other different religion—which is possible, as only 35 percent or so of all people on Earth consider themselves to be Catholic or some form of it as I have already mentioned—want to hear how your "God" is going to help them? Even though your heart may be in the right place, saying, "I will pray for you" is still not the way to go in my books.

Do you assume all people are heterosexual? Or are you careful about offending anyone around you when wanting to tell a "gay" joke, if you do at all. If you are someone who tells jokes about different races of people and so on, do you do so when someone of that race you are going to make fun of is there? I dislike all these types of jokes regardless of who is around, but many people are careful about offending others in these sorts of situations, aren't they. How is going on about "God" any different? Be politically correct here, will you please. And it deserves to be said again; any "joke" where you are making fun of an individual's sexuality, race, or anything else that makes him or her seem different or not as good as a "normal" person, whatever the hell that is these days, is in bad taste. The classless joke says more about the person telling it.

I find everything about nature peaceful; this is probably because nature isn't tainted by humans and is always true—unless you subscribe to the conspiracy theory that claims the United States has a secret satellite that is orbiting the Earth that can actually create hurricanes and the type of earthquakes that can spawn tsunamis. I have said that we never really know the truth, but this story was a bit hard for even me to believe. I think some people have seen too many disaster movies, but I guess anything is possible.

In China, however, the government does induce clouds to go into labor if they need rain. Chinese scientists can also get the opposite effect, firing some chemical into the clouds that actually makes the floating pillows dissipate into next to nothing.

The Chinese government actually performed this awe-inspiring operation during the 2008 Olympics to ensure a rain-free event. I think we are opening Pandora's box here, and this scares me. Nature never needed our help in elevating us to the top of the natural food chain, but yet, now, we know better than her? How arrogant are we?

I don't pretend to know if the secret hurricane satellite really exists, but I do believe we really only get to know what people in influential positions in our society want us to think we know. (I know it is not true and just a movie but watch the flick, *Wag the Dog.*) No thanks! I choose to think I know that I don't know what is going on, instead of letting others have the satisfaction of heaving the blinds over my twenty-twenty vision. I am no person's blind fool. I will seek out the truth in my own manner and not the way I am led to do so. Of course, does this mean I do not know anything at all? Road kill anyone?

This just in, *Wikileaks* has just published thousands of pages of secret government documents detailing the inner workings of many governments around the world. Stay tuned for more as details become available.

The Lack of Transparency

IS THIS GREAT OR what? I asked for people in positions of power—people we put there—to have to take lie detector tests so we would know what they were up to. And now we know. Of course, many governments are calling the releasing of these documents illegal, but hey, we pay your salaries, so pipe down or you'll be fired. Quit trying to scare me into thinking that, somehow, if I know what you're doing, I'm going to have to fear terrorists more or something. This makes no sense. You aren't afraid, so why would I be? Does being rich now also mean you're more fearless? You would be the first to hide under your desk, so listen here, you little weasel; if you're doing something illegal, scary, or even fun, and we are paying for it because it's happening during office hours, we deserve to know about it, so stop your whining.

Wanting a secret government makes as much sense as me voting for someone and hoping to never know what he or she is doing, which is why I do not vote anymore; this is what happens. I have integrity, and I do not condone this form of behavior. By voting you're saying that you think it is okay for your government workers to cheat you, lie to you, and otherwise mistreat you. Why agree to this? Who in your life would you allow to act like this toward you? Not many if anyone, I am sure. So why then would you allow people who you've probably never even met and whose salary you pay to mistreat you? Think about that.

Getting back to the whining about the release of these documents, I do have a solution for you, though, you ignorant, on-your-knees, Wall Street ball-sucking, people-chiding, hypocritical, two-faced lawmakers. If you don't want to be seen in a negative light by people who elected you into office, "DON'T DO BAD THINGS!"

Our world has become so screwed up that Jamie, from his armchair-like bed, has become the voice of reason; is that how bad things are? There is nothing worse than people crying wolf when the people who do so are the ones who put the wolf in the henhouse in the first place.

Talking about cries for safety, let's consider airline and airport security. I find it remarkable that the rules are so stringent these days that we are basically getting molested in the name of terror and people barely speak out about this. Fly and get felt up or take the bus—these are your choices in a free and democratic society? And people thought McCarthyism was bad. We will look back one day and realize that people were acting as paranoid as a stray cat on acid.

Airport security checks have never caught anyone with a bomb, so perhaps that is good. But six-year-olds are being patted up and down in the name of—what, safety? Don't we put people who feel up six-year-olds—it's only with the back of the hands in this case, so it's okay—in jail? In today's world, we are so fucked up we think kids are being used as instruments of mass destruction by terrorists? Why? Because we saw this in a movie once? Wow, are we ever lost!

And it's not just little girls who are being checked. So are people in wheelchairs and people with bladder problems, and the list goes on and on. Our fearless leaders think that elderly white people who have to wear adult briefs essentially are actually caring fluids that can blow up planes? This is possible. But guess what? Everything and anything is possible, so where is the moral line? When does it end? The scary picture—it never will. There will always be something, because fear governs and rich people fly on private jets.

Is it really terrorists who have created this situation where we are bombarded by alerts that pique our fear levels? Or was it our employees—the government—who created this problem because they want us to be drones living in a state of uncertainty so they can continue to rule with impunity and, sadly, with poor judgment? I think this is a very fair question for us citizens to ask. Of course, we are not supposed to ask anything at all because being a good citizen means following the Pied Piper like rodents pursuing the smell of the rotting remains of those who walked the path before them. I say screw that! Listen, you are not braver than me, smarter than me, or better than me, so go find someone else to try and scare and stop wasting my money and time.

There is no easy way to get people who create terror here on Earth to stop their campaign of aggression, as there will there will always people who are angry for some reason. But I think one simple step would help a great deal. If you want terrorism to drop around the world, quit trying to tell others how colas and other products are good for them and their way of living is bad or wrong. Pushing yourself on any country is no different than ramming yourself onto a stranger in a bar. The scene may be chaotic and the people are just trying to have fun, but push too hard to dance with someone or take him or her home, and he or she will push back, right? And believe me, I am not condoning terrorism. I am merely saying that perhaps there is more at play here than meets the eye. I want to keep all channels of communication open.

The bar scenario demonstrates how this works is at the micro level, of course, but it is no different if you look at the bigger picture. I thought we all learnt this in grade school, but I guess not. The United States government likes to make *morality* a reason for invading other countries. But when there are fifty million people hungry and living in poverty in your own country and your citizens can't say anything at all contrary to what my government employees are saying, I kind of start to question the whole morality take on things. Saying other countries should be doing anything other than what they are doing is no different than a person taking shots at someone else for whatever reason—it helps to justify what you believe in. But individuals can do what they want, can't they? If I want to be miserable, then that is my right. Let other countries be and let "God" sort them out. Isn't that the saying? What? Their "God" is not the right one? Sigh!

The problem of terrorism does not stop there, however. People in the United States reject their army being used as peacekeepers for the world, but a scenario that is, perhaps, closer to reality exists. These soldiers, are tools of easily agitated and aggressive rich white men who are just trying to make a buck? You can blame the President, the Senate or Congress, but in the end, following the money trail to the end is where you shall find the truth. Sorry, but this is pretty much true. Realize, though, that I did not say just rich white Americans. Read up on the "Bilderberg Club" or the "Committee of 300" for more information. These "frats" are quite interesting, to say the least. As a disclaimer, I have no idea if these frats have anything to do with world affairs, but I don't have any information that says they don't either, so …

This just in: Airports will now stop screening people naked and, instead, use a generic form of the body for everyone. Was that so hard? Chalk one up for the people!

Getting back to *Wikileaks*, the website's "fondler" is wanted by Interpol on rape charges back in Sweden. I had never heard of this guy until all of the "leaks," and now he is a "rapist." I don't want to make light of rape in any way, but this is quite the coincidence, to say the least. I guess we shall wait and see. But of course, we'll never really know the truth. OJ was innocent, Tyson was guilty, and the jury is still out on this one. What do you think? Oh, and I just heard he is now running for a seat in the Senate back in Australia? I can't possibly keep up.

As an aside, when you read up on those clubs and realize the power that they possibly could exert upon society, you'll see how easily they could make someone disappear. That said, Dominique Strauss-Kahn (DSK), the man accused of raping a woman and the former head of the International Monetary Fund has been released from prison now. But a man who had to rob a bank for a buck so he could get health care still sits in jail to receive his free health care? Rich people plea out of court, and economically challenged citizens are a problem for the middle class whose taxes pay for them to sit in jail. Nice! At least that one "criminal" has nice teeth now.

This just in, and like I just mentioned, I cannot possibly keep up. DSK is now being charged for being involved in a prostitution ring back in France.

Finally, back to the weather, now, where it is a little overcast and to getting my bed-pan changed while I am at it.

BACK TO NATURE

AS FOR STORMS THAT are not caused by humans or any other kind of natural disaster (which is a funny name for this type of phenomena, as these natural *events*, not disasters, formed our world as we see it today), like I said thirteen pages ago, it is sad that people lose their lives or things they feel are important to them—whether they really are or not. What is tragic as well is what happens after the storm.

What we humans are doing to Earth and to each other is much worse than what any hurricane or any other type of storm can do to it. We can fix storm damage—if of course you are part of the privileged group that has insurance and money. Stupid insurance companies! As for humans, I personally find it shameful when "news agencies" talk about the loss of life *and* the property damage in the same breath. How many times have you heard this on the news? "Hundreds dead and billions of dollars in damage as Hurricane Katrina ..."

As a word to the wise, perhaps people should not be living in areas where typhoons frequently visit and near active volcanoes. But why do people live where death by nature is a possibility? Perhaps they have no choice. It seems to me that it is always the disadvantaged who suffer most when nature comes alive. In fact, the ten largest natural disasters of all time (ranked by number of deaths) ravaged the poorest people of their respective countries—many farmers and fisherman. Do an internet search and type in "the world's top ten worst natural disasters" and look for yourself.

These unfortunate millions who were simply born into their situation in many and most cases, especially in third-world countries, lived next to the water in shantytowns or on the hillsides in mud and rock huts and so on because they had to. And, of course, their homes offered no protection from the elements. The rich are safe in modern homes or are working in earthquake-safe buildings, so we do not have to worry about them. But you bet we can worry about the property damage—thanks to the news.

Just as bad as focusing on property damage is when someone of "importance" dies and gets special press coverage because some people knew who this person was. If you are alive, you are my equal and if you are dead, I will "pray" for you, but thinking I should be sadder for one family because his or her son or daughter was famous is nuts. To hear about this person as if he or she were better than others, I think, is disgraceful to all those who also lost loved ones. But that's just me. Recently, Whitney Houston passed away, and people mourned her because she had a nice voice. But a guy living on the streets because he has a crack addiction is not worth the same amount of respect? He sure is! Everyone deserves the same amount! Sadly, most people look at someone living on the streets as a bum. Whitney had every possible outlet to seek help, and she did not make it, so cut the guy on the street some slack please.

Anyway, that was a little off topic. Getting back to people and natural disasters, I think governments all over the world need to get to work on protecting all their people—not just the ones with money. Sadly and pathetically in almost every country the opposite is true-money buy's government protection. Well-to-do individuals in the United States who are living in prosperous states like Florida or the Carolinas love residing next to the beaches but, of course, are also well insured, whereas those living in Louisiana and Mississippi are predominately poorer. When Katrina came rolling in, where was the government then? Florida gets pelted by a storm, and the help arrives without the blink of an eye. But when the Gulf gets slammed, forget about it.

Am I being too critical here or am I splitting hairs? Let's look into this a little more closely. Hurricane Betsy ravaged the ninth ward in New Orleans back in 1965. What did the government learn from this? What was done to prevent another disaster that was just waiting to happen? In this case, the disaster was Hurricane Katrina. Not enough for some obvious reason. People there are still waiting for insurance companies and charities that took in money to help them with their just aid—and I'm talking about the 1965 event. Pathetic! Not everyone can be Warren Buffet, but all people should be able feel safe in their homes no matter where they live.

As an aside, why, when we look at Mr. Buffett's life, do we overlook the fact that he had a wife out on the West Coast and a live-in girlfriend at his home in Omaha? I only point this out because society sure seems to be giving Charlie Sheen a headache about how he is living his life. Why the difference? Oh, of course, Chuck is a rebel, and Buffett is a nice guy. So shame on you, Charlie, for living your life the way you want. It may not be the best life for you based on what we think is good and healthy, but it is yours to do with as you please. So enjoy—and call me!

In my opinion, life means living and not just surviving. I think we all deserve to live and to live well. There is no reason why the superrich or well-off should not be able to enjoy the lifestyle that they do, but there is also no reason why some should have no food and literally be unable to get by on a day-to-day basis. Mitt Romney's kids have $100 million trust fund; good for them. But in the same country, thousands are living on the street, and millions are hungry. Politicians can't keep turning a blind eye to these people. They are potential consumers, right?

Anyway, this Marxist drift is getting away from storms and nature, so in order to tie everything neatly together, I will say… Hmmm … I want to talk about something else now. I am a smooth operator, like a star who lip-synchs a song on live television and gets caught doing it.

So where were we? Were we not heading to the grocery store? Well, considering that I have the entire day to do whatever I choose to do—within reason of course, as I am hardly in the condition to do anything overly bipedal—I believe I will change things up. I think I will head to the bookstore first and then, perhaps, do some grocery shopping after. Being as this is a story, I can do anything, right. Also, there is a saying I am sure you know: "Don't put off until tomorrow what you can do today." So to set an example, of course I will do the opposite.

The rain has now intensified. I ingeniously deduced this integral and life-saving fact by inquisitively leering not at the sky but at small Lake Hatchback located on the front passenger seat of my heap of rust on wheels. The seat is wet because the window on that side is down. It was down because I like the passenger side window open while cruising around and not the driver's side and, of course, because I forgot to close it. I prefer driving around like this because if the driver's side window were ajar, that would mean I would have to twist off the top and …

The real answer is, pathetically and a little on the embarrassing side, when I drive with the driver's side window open, my hair blows around uncontrollably and, thus, becomes messy, so in this story, my window was also down. Realism is important when telling a story, right. Also, I didn't point out that I stress about this first thing in the morning for no reason you know.

Anyhow, getting back to my fable, my side of the car is dry, so all is good. Luckily, in a sad and depressing way, the front passenger seat of my car is the same as the other side of my bed—always empty. I am alone but not lonely, so onward we go to be around others at the bookstore. Please come. I am not lonely but bored, so help out a dying man won't you.

I twist the key in "the Beast," and with a little hesitation and the grace of a one-legged cat participating in the Feline Special Olympics, she turns over. My car requires a little maintenance, but that will have to wait, as I now have no income to appease such desires. I said desires and not necessities because, in our world, we are bombarded by ads telling us what we need. But in reality, we humans do not need as much as we think.

It is amazing how weather affects people's driving as much as their moods. Seriously, people, it's not like we are driving on ice. With all these idiots out here, I'm happy to be finally driving into the bookstore parking lot.

THE BOOKSTORE: PART TWO

WELL WILL YOU LOOK at that—a parking spot right in front of the bookstore. I usually find this area "full," if this is even the right word, with the cars of employees, but I guess today is my lucky day. It's amazing how things appear to be flowing in a much more positive direction ever since I started writing as if that was, indeed, the direction in which my life is heading. Sadly, this hopeful tale could not be further from the truth. But for the story's sake, feeling free is making my life better for the time being. Just roll with that for now. Anyhow, let's get out from underneath the wrath of Mother Nature before the 35 percent of me that isn't water gets wet.

Ouch! Thanks for holding the door open, friend. Come here so I can jab you with the umbrella I wish I had, jerk! See, I am happier; no swearing. Anyway, in we go to the home of Descartes, Socrates, Shakespeare ... and Dennis Rodman? It goes to show you that anything can be a success if you want it to be—hint, hint! It's amazing that being good at grabbing balls and acting foolishly can make you millions and turn you into an author and pseudo celebrity. Sure, you money hungry publishers, it's all about the content and grammar. Your days are numbered to be sure, so bite me.

Not winning any points here, but, in my defense, I'm up against Rodman, so points are hard to come by. As an aside, Rodman is now coaching some topless women's basketball game or something like that. It must be nice to have no dignity and be able to just use people to make money—until these "stars" are irrelevant and make themselves look old, used, and ready to be thrown out, of course. Yes, I am talking about publishers again. How Rodman ever got a book published just blows my mind. No jealousy here at all.

Wow this place is quiet. It has an Elizabethan era feel to it today, which I think is kind of charming. By this, I mean the store has a quiet, yet still romantic feel to it today. And, I said I hated the idea of *royal families* and not necessarily time periods in history, so quit trying to poke holes in my solid line of logic and reasoning. Okay, even I could not keep a straight face on that one.

Moving along, while laughing out loud, I deem the tranquility of this place worth mentioning, as most days here at the bookstore, kids are running around like it was their personal playground. So I am just appreciating the energy it has today. I do love seeing children having unabated fun—I really do—but not here when I am trying to relax and read. I know this is not a library, but it's not a gym either, right? Right!?

You might be wondering if everything has to revolve around me. Sure, why not!? Why shouldn't I set my own sail and do or think what is best for me? How could anyone live otherwise? You are your own ultimate boss. If you deal with what life throws your way while holding this point of view and not one where you are tossed about like a shrimp in a salad, you can be the main course in life and not the cocks' tail. Bottoms up!

This does not literally mean you need to turn everything that's not up to your standards into some sort of life-and-death struggle as I seem to do. But it does imply that it's okay to speak your mind. You may, from time to time, run into resistance from a kid's parent when you tell her to tell her kid to shut up. But if you don't like what's going on around you, you really do only have two choices in terms of your response. You can say something or you can "take it." I guess the third scenario is you can be okay with it, but that's too weird to comprehend. If someone is bothering you, I think at the very least you should stick up for yourself and say something. You may not be liked but you will be respected, which in my books, is better—unless you do things my way. I like a number of people in the world, but I truly only respect a few. And *shut up* is kind of harsh, but I think you know I was just trying to make a point and would never say that. It was, "Please shut the fuck up" for the record!

Personally, on the subject of swearing, I think we need to rethink how we define acceptable language and good manners. Is the word *fuck* really so bad? I have tried not to use it but I can only say *screwed* and *messed up* so many times. We can watch people getting literally mentally fucked in our society daily, but saying this four-letter profanity is bad? I do not fucking think so. When you can turn on the news and watch babies dying of starvation and people being blown up, I think we have bigger problems than worrying about such insignificant things.

Earlier, I eluded to my belief that throwing "trash" onto the concrete—ground that was once helping the environment but is now a slut that has been laid out to be driven over and over again— is bad. But how crazy is this? We have all these rules by which we are supposed to live, but, really, if there is one more thing I "have to do," I will ... have to move on. The lines of reason and good taste may be further away than they appear; this has been branded on to my mental rearview mirror. Read into that as you will.

I could be mistaken, but this is how I feel. Call me Freud and sue me as I postulate about life based on my own experiences and education. I will say that again—call me Freud! If you don't know anything about him, then you may not get what I am saying here. However, as I've already shown time and time again, it is easy to find things out if you want to. Fine, a great number of Freud's conclusions about humans were based on his personal experiences but turned out to be wrong.

Regarding kids, is it incorrect or selfish of me to want them to refrain from darting around the bookstore for whatever reason? No, it is not wrong; maybe it's a little "small-minded," but it's not a thought or feeling that's wide of the suitable mark as most know that to be I think. Or is it? How the hell would anyone really be able to know? Officials, I need a ruling!

In our world, and I mean our personal worlds, we all like to think we know how to act or behave properly, but look at what I said—our personal worlds. How can anyone else know my personal world? Do we all have the same moms and, more to the point, minds? We all think we realize and comprehend the differences between good and bad behaviors, but those parameters of understanding differ from person to person and, thus, are truly impossible to know. We judge the hell out of people when we see they are not the same as us, but this is absurd behavior. We can generalize, but this takes us back to making assumptions, and of course, assumptions can be off the mark sometimes, if not most of the time. So just follow me.

Do I have your vote? Better me than Edwards, don't you think? He spent $1 million to cover up an affair while running for president of the United States. At the same time, sadly, many people loved his populous platform. Sure, he was there for all of you. Of course, as I've been saying about what you think you know, no one really knew him, did they? Yet, while this is true, many people were hoping he would become the president of the United States of America? As you have probably read, he has since been indicted. But do you think he will do jail time? I doubt it! And as for his "for the people platform," well, it went up in smoke like a joint in jail does—illegally. Have fun, Senator "Eddy."

Definition time:

Blind faith: (1) a sober person's drunken stupor; (2) a drunken person's dream.

As an endnote about John Edwards, he was recently diagnosed with a heart problem that requires surgery. He may be a liar, but I don't wish harm on anyone, so I hope it goes well.

Another characteristic that makes living in our society hard is that most of us are raised to run around the track with blinders on like a doped-up horse at a chariot race. Thus, it's easy to lose sight sometimes of the simplest of things—like, for example, being kind to one another. "Thanks for holding the door open for me" is an all too common thing I hear. From time to time, though, we all forget to open the door for someone else, don't we? Or sometimes we say something that comes across as mean because, at that moment, our focus is so acute, we are ignorant of other people's perceived needs and desires. How many times can you recall doing something that you briefly regretted?

This is not to say that we shouldn't focus on what we're doing or that what we're engaged in is less important than what someone else is up to. But at the same time, we shouldn't think what we're doing is more vital than what someone else feels is just as essential to him or her. As for how this relates to me and my dislike for kids running around, it would be first class of me if I could imagine I was a parent who was cooped up in my home for two weeks due to my child being sick in bed, as this could easily be the case for some of these "neglectful" parents right. Then, perhaps, I could understand why the parents of these little gerbils could let their children scamper around like they were on a miniature jungle gym in a cage—it just feels great to get out from beneath that mentally challenging situation they were in. This would be so nice of me, right?

But, NO; I cannot get there! I hate kids running around the bookstore, and it is my right to feel this way. I can feel and think any way I want, as it is my life. I am not responsible for someone else's crappy life, so stop bothering me. There are consequences attached to not wanting to open up my mind, but I haven't been able to see the possible ramifications of such thinking; nor have I wanted to, so here we are. I've never cared if my blood pressure rested at 240/140. I have lived by the phrase, if you try to chase two rabbits at the same time, both will get away. The point or meaning of this phrase is, if you concentrate on just one prize, you will be more successful.

So, for the rest of this story I will do just that—focus on me. Although this philosophy has the stench of success and is not far from what I always did, I am good at this, so forward we go.

Definition time:

Reality (1) a conjured up and evilly manifested idea of the rich for the delusional amusement of my branded mind; (2) my nightmare.

I do feel that being a little balanced is better than having laser-like focus, as that makes for a more interesting and fulfilling life.

But I just can't seem to do that. I am so compulsive. Once I start something, that's it for me—either go hard or go home. There seems to be no middle ground for me, even though I am aware of my obsessive and neurotic tendencies. Maybe I can find myself yet another book to read that claims to have all the answers for helping people to see the light. Or, I could seek professional help; but for two hundred bucks an hour, I had better get some wining, dining and … ego shining as well or, at the very least, results that last longer than my attention span.

As an aside, did you think I was going to say something else there? I may be crooked, but I am not a literary crook. Alanis Morissette said something like that in one of her great songs back in the nineties for the record. Puns are falling like my pulse—rapidly.

"Emergency in room F!"

Getting back to the story and away from reality, we are just talking about feeling happy here and not the ridiculousness of our world, so maybe I should relax. That would be novel of me. Of course, does thinking about my life and the world that I see mean I am not relaxed? Why would that be? It's not like I'm going out and killing people. Maybe those who tell others to relax should chill, as using your brain is not a bad thing. I may not love soup as much as my "bra," but so what? At least I am entertaining and have original thoughts in my head. How do you like them apples? There will be more about stealing other's ideas a little later on this hunt, "God" willing.

I do like bookstores, though, as just seeing the plethora of books reminds me of how much there is to know about our world. For example, there are books related to or on anthrophobia, carnophobia, ecclesiophobia, and even hobby books that talk about things like gardening. History books can teach us about where we came from and, thus, help us to understand who we are today. I hate history books, though—boring!

Anyhow, feeling inspired and open to possibilities, I contemplate reading for free and then maybe even buying a self-motivation book. I say self-motivation and not self-help like we talked about back on page sixty-something or so, because in the past, anyway, I found most motivational books to be informative, as there were words in them; but the books did not get me revved up as much as my will to do so did. I am not a robot. I can't be expected to follow what seems to be the norm—seven rules and then become happy—can I? My six steps in the morning are already hard enough for me to do without losing my mind.

Personally, I want a book that allows me to be me, a person who is already great. I don't want to learn how to get things I desire by mirroring others, when, to do so, I have to become someone I am not. To me this seems more about deceit than anything else. I am no chameleon. On the other hand, chameleons have been successful and around for a long time, so maybe there is something to be said about being flexible. Of course, however, I am as rigid as blades on a chipper, so on to the other side of the argument I go. As usual, my mind makes this real and nothing else. Anyway, full steam ahead now as I commandeer this runaway locomotive tangent away from insanity and toward reason. I said toward and not into, for the record.

I chug around like a turtle racing a sloth in the Boston Marathon—and this is full steam for me—before getting up enough courage to head for the psychology/self-help section. Weird how just possibly reading something takes courage. I decide to grab that dumb, *D-Day* death book. I always did actually like and respect Heather, so if she liked this book, it must be okay, right?

I am so indecisive. I am always looking for, in my bogus rhetorical "right" question, super reinforced backing for what I am thinking by those who can never truly understand my thoughts or ideas. These people who "help" me may also be wrong, but I allow them to cast my sail and send me adrift. Anchors away please, captain! Sadly, my anchor is away, far away—as in back on land.

If I had more confidence, would I need such reassurances from those who I have not even met before? I think in day-to-day life the answer would be no, as needing other people's brains to "make" you sense you feel better about what you are doing is about as logical as doing a thousand bicep curls at the gym every day to get you ready for the Tour de France. If the event was full contact bike riding, this may help, but ...

In the end, no matter what you think anyone has told you, you are the one who is making all of the decisions for your life. You are already confident but perhaps simply do not realize it. Reflect on what I have just said. Did you think about that? If you did, do you feel you did so because I told you to? No! You chose to do it. You made the decision. I just suggested it. Think about that!

Regarding Heathen—hmmm, close enough—I said many not-so-great things about her a while back, didn't I? Of course, that was just a pathetic and, at best, semitransparent cover for trying to hide my own inner problems, which I am not yet comfortable with or even conscious of due to my having convenient attention deficit disorder, or CADD. Here comes another bout of this crippling disease now...

Where were we? Oh, it's now time to read. The book starts off with the cover and some nice art and ... Oh my goodness; help me!

D-Day

SO, *D-DAY* TO THIS author stands for desire, discipline, dedication, and determination; cool, but so what? This is kind of like the motivational guy who made the acronym POW into something like the "power of working." That hardly seems right. Anyway, *D-Day* was interesting, and surprisingly, I think I understand what the crazy author is trying to say—that we really need to wake up to the reality beyond our senses. And I'm not thinking just of people in the West; I mean all individuals. Everyone everywhere should become more aware of how our thinking limits not only our development on a personal level but also on a global one. Hey, I could have written this book.

I believe cultural devotion is at the root of many of our problems today, even though no one really talks about this. We are told to be proud of our heritage, but really, why? Having been born in any one country is no accomplishment, and my parents always told me I was an accident so...

Seriously, we are raised to be patriotic, but patriotism comes at a price. Patriotism creates an us-versus-them scenario, which is of no benefit to most; after all, there can only be so many winners, and those are the top few percent on the totem pole of wealth. "Leaders" of our world try to claim what they are doing is positive for all, but to be sure, the civilians on the ground being murdered, robbed, starved, turned away from hospitals because they have no insurance, and so on don't care about rich people trying to get richer. However, we have to live this way as this is life as we know it, isn't it? I said this earlier, but the revolution is coming. This nonsense has to come to an end because patriotism is really only helping out those who do not need any help.

This social dynamic, patriotism, actually gets in the way of any real societal or personal progress, as we are not utilizing all of the skills we have been given to the fullest of our natural abilities. Because of how society has been set up, most people must act out the role of the "worker bee," which creates brain-dead soldiers and unhappiness. But this is patriotism at work. This—taking one for your country—is not a very fulfilling way to have to live, is it. Investing more directly in people would create the wealthiest of countries—fiscally, mentally, and spiritually. Fiscally came first there because, let's face it, money wins the gold in our world whether we like it or not; every country is in a fight to create jobs so it can generate more wealth.

For those few who we do not know yet still run the world, promoting the bearing of the flag is vital because it promotes nationalism. This, of course, drives many economies and, thus, renders a few shrewd people very well-off. . Then, this fortunate minority tries to protect what they have by spoon-feeding people the lie of how imperative practicing the art of jingoism is for themselves and their country. Sorry, but I never choose where to be born, so how can I or why should I put much stalk in "*my*" country—especially when it doesn't result in a reasonable job for me. Because I have been brain washed to do so?

Oh yes, now I remember—I have to or else I am the enemy. I cannot say this enough; actually, I give up. I was going to say that we do not have to be the pawns in life, but what can people do? We are so thoroughly overruled on every call that, even if we are up forty love in the game of life, game point always goes to the machine. I think freedom should have the letter *e* at the end of it, as that would make more sense. Free-dome—like free but with a low ceiling.

Definition time:

Freedom: Do as I say, and you are free to do what you have been told.

On a planet wide level, our education should be more global in nature and focus on the similarities of our species instead of the differences. When I meet people anywhere in the world, I unequivocally think I am meeting a person just like me. Puff, puff, and pass, my friend, because while this person may have his or her own view of the world, the floating mass of knowledge that he or she subscribes to is based upon where he or she was born and nothing more. When what one learns is not a choice, why do the differences in that education seem so important? I do not get that? You can think "your" country is better than someone else's, but this line of thinking truly will never lead to anything positive, so why bother? Be grateful if you do live in a safe and prosperous country, but don't boast about it. As an aside, I do think stoning and behavior such as this is wrong, but this is only because smoking pot is illegal.

I wonder why I feel I have to settle down in the country in which I was born. What keeps me here—my dream? What a grand vision it is for my one and only life. The dream is, again, if I follow the rules of my society and work hard, I can live the life that society wants me to think is desirable or, even better, have a house, a car, a vacation once a year, and maybe even a good partner who actually loves me. This is what we strive for while we, "happily" for appearances sake, have to fear everything else in our world. What a joy—especially when there are no jobs that pay enough to get me my house, my vacation, my car, and all the rest.

Your, "in-flight delusion," like mine, is your fate. This may not be ghastly, but if your dream is based or founded on the ideas of how others want you to see your own reality, be careful! Given that so many people are stressed-out and unhappy, perhaps it is time to really look at what this real-life wake is doing for most of us and then strive for something better. Can most of us be wrong? And I say most of us because not everyone appears to be stressed-out or unhappy, you freaks!

Sadly, I have never done anything to improve my situation. I wanted to, but Captain Crook's iron claw had too firm a grip on me. The fear of trying to buck the system like a bull does a cowboy has rendered me pretty much useless because the unknown scares me. I feel braver now, but back in the days, I thought that, if I stayed in my igloo, I could control the temperamental climate. So I always did just that—I remained "ice-olated." (Come on, you have to give me that one!)

Anyway, was I not feeling free or something like that? My analytical style and persistent flashbacks gets the better of me sometimes. My apologies! On with my story—our story!

I am now feeling free for the first time since I was a kid. Even then I remember having problems with others and so on, so scratch that. Still, perhaps this is the start of the Jamie revolution.

Talking about kids, did you know that six-year-olds laugh on average about three billion times per day, while adults do so somewhere between never and rarely? The older we get, the wiser we are supposed to be. But isn't laughing a good thing? Laughing increases the amount of positive endorphins your body secretes, and these little balls of joy have been linked to better health. But we need to be responsible, right? Well, you can keep on reading if for no other reason than you are getting a chuckle out of my slow demise because it is good for your health.

A friend of mine gave me some advice about being happier that I should have taken sooner. She told me—back when I had a spine— that if I was tired of getting screwed, I should stop masturbating (or being the "master's bait") because in the end, we are only screwing ourselves. However, while the idea of our lives being our own responsibilities may be true to a degree, blaming others makes sense as well—for nearsighted individuals anyway—as doing so allows you to feel better then and there. The long-term prognosis may not be great, but maybe I will be hit by a bus tomorrow; long-term thinking isn't conducive to feeling good now, so blame away I say. The pleasure and benefits one gets by playing the blame game may be as productive and useful as sticking a Band-Aid on your head for your war-torn, illogical mind, but do what you think you have to do. By the end of this story, you may want to rethink some of the things I have spewed; but for now, blaming is in.

At any rate, it is time to move on. Let's turn to a different page.

While that was an interesting read, I was getting a little bored, and to be honest, I have no idea what I am talking about anymore. Here we go.

Yes! Wow! Even though I already "know" this is my life to enjoy and do with as I please, it is still nice to know I am on the right course (did the book really say this?). Of course, I have no job now and no means by which to make money, so vacationing is out of the question (I am way off the mark—yet, again!) but my time will come. The source that provides the light of life in my world, money, is sucked out and away from me like water before an impending tsunami—efficiently.

As for vacationing, a friend of mine once told me that our lives are the "trip of a lifetime." Sadly, though, my chartered boat always seems to be sinking. I understand that I am only here one time in this vessel and I should try to enjoy the breeze of life whenever possible, but not having any free time makes that difficult. I always seem to be working so I can try and make the dream happen. I am like a dog trying to catch its tail. I have worked hard for almost fifteen years already, and I have nothing to show for it—not including my belly, of course. It has been well compensated. Sure, I have a degree on my wall, but even though it is bigger than a dollar bill, it is actually worth less somehow. Read into that as you will. While you are at it, do an Internet search for the following— "society's biggest scam, post secondary education."

It's getting late now, and I still have to go buy a few items from the grocery store. It's amazing how time flies when you are engaged in something interesting. So, the question of the moment is, should I stay or should I go now?

I decide to stay for a little longer and try to believe that the world is my oyster and I am not bound by time. I flip to the back of the book, looking to read something that does not make me think too much. I want to relax and enjoy my newfound life. Even in freedom, there are conditions to abide by. Think about that.

Dry, true, and another wasted piece of paper comes and goes like the daily newspaper does these days. That sums up what I just read. Just as well, as it is past getting late now, and I still have to go groceries shopping. I would like to read more but some other time. I could, I guess, purchase this monstrosity of a book and read it leisurely at home, but oh my God, without the 800 percent tax added on, it's already twenty-five bucks. I have no job, so how in the world can I ever afford this life-saving death book?

We always seem to stay "within our comfort zones." But what a crazy phrase that is, as I think most people want to jump out of their skins all the time. What comfort zone? One day without a job and I am already worried that I have no money to buy a book? A regular income is comfortable for my mind, even if I am miserable while making that happen. Think about that—if you feel the same as me I guess. If you disagree, stay within your comfort zone and move on. But it's hard for me to imagine that anyone likes going into work to make a few bucks a year while the CEO makes one zillion times what you do or more. What is worse is that this person—your boss, who is a twit and dumber than you—was, more than likely, born into money so *he* had a lot less travelling to do to get where he is. I work my ass off to just get to the middle. And I am in the top 50 percent of people when it comes to IQ, but because of the situation I was born into, life is harder for me. That sucks. Looking back, though, I wish someone would have gotten the violin out for me and started playing, but sadly, that never happened. Ignorance has no friends.

Anyway, it is time to move on. I guess since I can't afford anything anymore, I will just come back here tomorrow and read for free. What a plan. Let's get out of here.

Business and More Purging

AS I PUT THE book back and slowly walk up to the front of the store, I recall, for some reason, a time I saw Bob here. He was reading some medical magazine. Suddenly, before I knew it, a blasting, "Jamie, how are you?" roared across my bloated belly loud enough to stop everyone in the sunken tracks of those who stood there after me.

He was very excited to see me, which seemed strange to me because I barely knew him at the time. I had met him just once before while visiting a hospital for an undisclosed reason that I am going to keep that way.

Anyway, I walked over, curious as to what he was doing. So I asked, "What are you doing here, Bob?"

"I am here to meet my friend, Pete. He just lost his job and is feeling a little down, so I am meeting him here to lend an ear, console if necessary, and to try and cheer him up. How are you? How are you feeling?" Bob finished up, prodding me like a cow with a cholesterol problem.

"I'm okay. Same, same, Bob," I replied.

As Bob and I spoke more about his friend than about me, the meeting made me realize that, worldwide, huge mergers were increasing in order to help businesses remain "competitive," all the while doing nothing for the people who worked at the those companies. Just a couple years past an economic meltdown and not even out of the patch of clear-cut moral wrongs, business owners in the United States were giving themselves huge pats on the back— as if they're their own best fans—as well as millions of dollars in bonuses. Heck, some of the bailout money they received from the taxpayers was set aside for bonuses. Money well spent right, as we all know how great a job our business leaders are doing—at ripping people off.

And again, I am not saying that being wealthy is a bad thing. However, when rich guys are committing the biggest crimes in the world, maybe it's time to stop looking the other way and hold them accountable for the mess *our* world is in. Of course, they control every avenue in which to pursue such a cause, even the dynamics of what is acceptable in their society, so be prepared for a long battle or, more likely, going bankrupt.

As for Bob's friend, sadly, he was a casualty of globalization— the new/old baby of the rich. Bob's buddy had become a statistic in a mainframe computer in some government building basement and nothing more. Welcome to our insane world, where most people are forced to work like sled-pulling dogs while having to avoid the whips as we run through the gauntlet of life—our lives.

Our current era reminds me, from what I know about it, of the period when the advent of the Industrial Revolution was taking the world by storm. People, humans were treated like bears in a circus. They worked hard and were thrown an organ or two for their troubles while, at the same time, a small percentage of "important" citizens reaped huge financial rewards. The bear lived in cages and was shackled while the "elite" lived in mansions. It wasn't until the people broke free of their mental chains and chose to roam free that change began. Laws were put in place to help protect the pawns—or keep them where they already were if you want to be contemptuous. But things were a little better at least, even if just on paper, than they had been.

As I mentioned a little earlier, mergers are happening at record paces with copious amounts of money changing hands at the top while those at the bottom are bowled over and laid to rest like sardines in a tin can. Before one knows it, there will be twenty companies running the world and people will be bound tighter than a thousand pounds of trinitrotoluene in one small stick of dynamite. Is this really what we want—to be fighting for scraps and leftovers? Are we animals? We pretend to be civilized, yet we cut each other up with words just as viciously as seals get clubbed on the head. So if the aforementioned were to happen, could you imagine what people would do to secure a job?

Mad Max is coming! I am sorry to say, but the eradication of civility, jobs, and even countries has already begun. We need to change course and quickly!

Today, because of "conservative ideology" and globalization—which, as an aside, is a phony word, as when hasn't trading been global in nature—people are not only losing their jobs, they are also losing their pensions and their security. Normal citizens have been force-fed to the belief that entities like pensions and securities exist when you work hard, but what I see are promises full of holes. What follows is natural in our world; without jobs there is no money. This, we end up with a percentage of our population that suffers from low self-esteem and is unemployed and economically challenged.

Unemployment is high, and guess what? It won't get much better anytime soon because companies are trying to stay competitive. Sadly, people expect much from life if they've done what they've been told to do, but in the end, our system is broken and aided only by Scotch tape. So screw what you have been taught, as that is not the way, it is someone else's idea for you and nothing more.

Working hard for money, buying stuff so you feel good about yourself, drinking and smoking to relieve stress, and so on are symptoms of a bigger problem in our world. So while you are responsible for your life, so are others, and for too long, they have received a free pass. But no more. I say everyone should quit his or her jobs and see what happens then. This is my solution for those who are not living the dream.

Now, considering this is coming from a guy who never took his own advice and lived with questionable morals and habits, take what I have said here with a grain of salt. I am just bitter because my life has always been so hard. I am trying to show another side now, however—a position that contrasts just being negative. But in reality, it's too late for me. I just hope you're getting what I'm saying. If you are still in the dark, don't worry; everything will become clear in the end.

As I try to relax, I realize there is a lot of commotion all around me. My heart begins to beat even faster now. We need to hurry.

THE AIRLINE INDUSTRY

TALKING ABOUT ECONOMICS AND how sick things are, let's look at the airline industry for a minute. The airline industry is for the economy what a frog is for the environment—a good indicator of how good or bad things are. Companies today are folding, merging, cutting staff, and slashing workers' pay in order to stay competitive. But when does this end?

Eventually, the airline industry in every developed nation will follow that of Canada. One major player will emerge simply because it is bigger than the other airlines and able to endure losing money for longer. And then, *bam*, that company will hike fees and dominate with impunity. Flying the friendly skies will be like what it was fifty years ago—affordable only for the affluent. With the gap between the rich and the poor growing like the population would if it were near the Fukushima Nuclear Reactor Plant—sickly—this idea of mine is not so farfetched. People without resources now are about as likely to become well-off and successful as two rapid ligers who are trying to reproduce.

As an aside, when airlines hiked fees because of the record high cost of fuel (when oil was around $150 a barrel), why did they not drop them when the cost of fuel went down? Now we are paying in order to bring bags on board and for sandwiches and drinks. Is there any other industry that could operate like this and get away with it? Heck, just the other day, some pilot threw two men off of the airplane because they were Muslim. The two were screened, taken off the airplane, and screened again, but even still the pilot refused to fly with them. What is next, a Catholic pilot throwing an atheist off a flight? Welcome to the new world!

As for Air Canada and to show another example of how

business people are taking care of themselves first, in order to stay in the skies over the years, the workers there have had to endure huge cuts across the board on many occasions. However, the previous CEO, Robert Milton, took home over $86 million dollars in salary and bonuses while employees were forced to take a $10,000-dollar pay cut during that same time. Now, the new CEO, Calvin Rovinescu, is asking for more cuts, while at the same time, he has generously bestowed upon himself a 76 percent pay hike and a luxurious retirement package. Yet, he sits and talks about how the company needs to cut pay. These people look you in the face and just lie. Fudge you, buddy! I want to say something funny here, but I would rather punch this guy in the face, so I have nothing.

The global economy could be a good thing in theory if the rules were the same for everyone, but when only Baltic and Mediterranean are for sale and you have just passed them and are headed for hotel-riddled properties with an empty wallet, it's pretty hard to enjoy the game, isn't it? There should be a mercy rule like in baseball or softball—once you get to far ahead, you can no longer accumulate more runs. We should do this with money, with the surplus being spread out among those with zero. What, you can't live with only $1 billion? Okay, I understand. You want all of your money to sit and do nothing because you never know when you will need to buy a billion-dollar food stamp.

There are some nice bosses out there to be sure, but most are on ego trips and are stuck playing king of the mountain instead of doing what is best for the company; at least this is what I have experienced. Slavery was abolished a long time ago, but really, society has always been about cheap labor. And while the appearance of society has changed, it is, sadly, very much the same as it ever was. If you are not making "master" happy, the phrase "watch out" still applies, doesn't it? And no, I am not making light of slavery, the past, or anything like that. I am so tired of having to justify myself, I am just going to move on.

You know, people don't take our power away—we give it away. I am merely speaking the truth, yet I have to justify my every word. Why?

Back to crappy business facts that piss me off.

In January 2009, I read in the newspaper that some CEO's gobbled up over $200 million dollars in severance pay. And like I just said, CEO's are now raiding the cookie jar again, just a few years removed from when they were trying to look humble and like everyone else, actually driving to meetings instead of taking private jets. All this when it was just reported that another recession upon us. Businesspeople, or as I like to call them, paper pushers, help themselves to whatever they want, don't they? A CEO's wage in 2010 in the United States was 343 times the average wage, and they took in over $3 billion dollars-enough to cover the salaries of over one hundred thousand full-time jobs.

The CEO of GE, was paid over $21 million dollars in compensation last year. This is on top of his yearly salary. Is this crazy or what? Hey boss dude, listen up; it is the employees that will make or break your company, not you, you self-absorbed roach, so take care of your employees, and they will take care of you. The idea that you should be rewarded when things go well but not be held responsible if they don't makes as much sense as paying taxes so allied leaders in Afghanistan and Iraq can live a charmed life.

If you want your company to stay competitive, forget the $200 million bonus you enjoy offering yourself CEO person, and hire a whack of employees and let them all do less than what they would normally have to do. Then, watch productivity go up, as your workers would actually enjoy the job more and, thus, take less sick days and so on. You could create the happiest workplace in the world. Creating this type of environment would not only be amazing, it would be commendable as well. And I am not saying that, because of the "extra" labor force, the prices of your goods should go up. They would not; nor should they. Don't be greedy.

Idealistic I know, but why not? Why shouldn't we do what is good for the majority in this case? Is this not how our world is run—in theory anyway? "Tyranny of the majority" is the system that governments seem to operate by these days. But when it comes to finances, things work in the opposite direction—the minority with the most rule. Why is that? We are the other 99 percent.

Personally, I think that running a company in this way would make the customers happy as well as the employees. And in a market that is hurting for business, doesn't having people working make sense? Yes, the "haves" are saying no. That has been noted!

Of course, with all the competition out there, any company with extra labor would be destroyed in no time. However, I like the idea. This may just be the future of our world, though. When you look at China's pseudo socialist system and even most countries in Europe where the taxes are so high most people net about the same amount of Euro whether you are a doctor or a trash collector, it's not hard to picture this scenario growing into reality. Having people working is a good thing for everyone. The problem everywhere is a lack of jobs, which brings me back to my suggestion to hire more employees. The suggestion, of course, is as likely to be picked up as I am to pick up on an all the women at nude beach, but oh well.

As for executives' bonuses, how many people out there would support a bill banning businesspeople from getting bonuses? People who receive gifts are not allowed to do so tax-free, so why do these knuckleheads get to have all this free money? Yes it is taxed—maybe—but you know what I mean.

Anyway, enough about business facts that make me as sick as a bulimic anorexic with multiple personalities, as the more I talk about this, the greater my desire is to find sanity in a bowl of rat poison.

As for Bob's friend, I did feel badly for him at the time, but with my own problems I had shortly thereafter—my hair was beginning to recede—I really couldn't think much about him. We care when in public, but for how long would you have thought about this person?

It is time to leave this literary world. We have no time to spare. Onward we go with the story, as I open my eyes to the light that marks the end of my tunnel. Confusion and mayhem is all around me now, and I try to hold on just a little longer. My heart is doing its best, but the brain knows what is to come.

Stop Complaining

I PART THE ONE of the two doors that is not locked and wonder, *Why even have two if you are going to constantly keep one sealed shut?* Experiences and opportunities that are present in life are constantly being tapered down like my dying body—one hinge or artery at a time. A little drastic there perhaps, but the closed door was meant to symbolize the shrinking of the opportunity pool.

As I squeeze past some guy who is charging in, I instantly recognize something that is not quite right. As an aside, people, when using public transportation, those who are on board should get off *before* those waiting to board get in. Wait for people to get off of the elevator or the subway and then amble on. No offense, but I don't get off on exchanging clothing particles or smelling your breath as we grind our way to the other side. So let me off first or I will drop you to the ground with my shoulder like a soccer player hits the grass when being touched by a feather—without dignity or any trouble.

Anyway, I could be wrong but I believe it isn't proper for pickup trucks to be humping the back of cars. This probably has worked as well as a dead kitten helps a hypochondriac feel better, so call me Humpty as taking great falls is how I roll. In any case, I seem to have the worst luck with cars, trucks, people, and life.

Regarding this situation, though, I must admit that I have not been completely honest with you. I actually utilized two parking spots today, so whatever has happened is likely my fault—not that I want to admit that to "Farmer Boy." I thought, because I was feeling so great, I would treat my Betsy to her dream of wanting to feel like a star and consent to her desire to rest in two car beds,

but a lot of good that did me. Damn karma—yet again! Tick ...
tick ....tick ... goes my beat of life.

Anyhow, our conversation goes something like this:

"What happened?" I ask accusingly.

"Is this your car, jackass?" comes the reply from the not-so-jolly
giant.

"Yeah it is."

(More great reading or what? I still make Rodman jealous,
though.)

"Why did you take up two spots, especially when your car
is such a piece of crap? What makes you so special, you ignorant
imbecile?" this crazed man carries on.

I know where this lovely talk is going—to the land of self-
destruction, where I am the almighty ruler (if one can actually be
mighty in this pathetic place). He is extremely angry, and on top of
that, I get the feeling I could talk circles around him with a three-
word vocabulary so, I decide to try some hidden wisdom that was
locked up inside my subconscious. Having to remember you are
happy is hard to do moment to moment you know! "I was parked
in two spots, and you somehow were still stupid enough to hit me,
so what do you want to do about this? This unfortunate incident
was my fault, even though you can't drive, and I am sorry."

I am not sure where this calmness arose from but it definitely
defused his anger. Actually, he seemed a little confused by this
action.

In any case, after a little constructive dialogue instead of my
usual destructive banter, we both agreed that forgetting about this
little case of bump me, hump me, and dump me was in the best of
both of our interests—especially after I forked up the cash for a
seven-dollar cup of cancer fighting/causing coffee. In the end, the
moral of the story is, it is better to have loved and lost than to have
been punched out, especially when you were also in the wrong.

Moving on, to what or where I do not know—which makes
me think for about one second, am I really moving on? What do

you expect after one second—me mentally splitting the atom? Anyway, am I really living is a better question. I am trying to make myself think that I am, but is mindless chatter really living? Can one even engage in mindless chatter? Is it possible I will stop asking questions that I have no desire to answering, merely pushing back the inevitable, which is us moving on, by the way? Thinking is great, but over pondering about inconsequential things is as beneficial to your life as a bottle of whiskey is to a dead alcoholic, so mind your time wisely.

Beep goes the car as it passes by my left side. That was close. Patience, everyone, and get out of my way, as I have no intention of waiting for you to pass. As for beeping, I would have to say, because this book is too short and I need one more page filled, that South Korea is the beep capital of the world. South Koreans take the gold when it comes to honking their horns. China would be second, with the Philippines third. Of course, I have not been to that many countries or cities, so now I am acting like an eighty-year-old woman who has lived in a cave her whole life and making assumptions that will surely be wrong. I am such an "idiot servant" or something like that.

So where was I (and I do not mean geographically)? Oh yes, we were talking about complaining, right? No? Well, that's where we're going, so stop complaining. Have you ever stopped to think about what complaining is? A thesaurus will give only negative terms for the word *complaining,* among them belligerent, unreasonable, and argumentative. Most of us are taught when we are young that complaining is bad and that we should not engage in such unsavory behavior, but belligerent? This is too harsh and so off the reasonable mark that if I were an archer using *belligerent* as a synonym for *complaining,* it would be the equivalent of me missing the bull's-eye and hitting … hmmm, something else that by definition is not considered to be a bull's-eye.

At any rate, most people in our world are taught that the philosophical notion we call complaining is not the grandest or the best of actions one can engage in. As usual, I want to ask what makes this idea right, proper, or even logical? What is complaining?

Complaining really is just a way of sharing information, isn't it? Why is this so bad? Find the positive, right? How many times have you heard at work that you should "stop complaining"? Take it or you are unemployed is pretty much the way office politics works, isn't it? I suggest, that you don't listen to the I'm-too-busy shrug off or the stop-complaining banter; fire away. Be like a kid who just keeps asking and get whatever it is that you want, even if that is just the satisfaction of being heard. Speak your mind, boy!

Why is asking for something or sharing an opinion so bad—especially when, most of the time, what is being asked for is simply greater fairness? Why is the fact that most of us need to complain just to be heard not addressed in our society? Complaining in our "modern world" is similar to begging in the past, like a peasant to the kings. When people in "developed nations" are forced to beg, by way of complaining, for an adequate way of life, isn't this a cause for concern?

Realize, everyone complains—even leaders of the "Free World." The United States government is constantly complaining about the Chinese currency being "undervalued," aren't they? Sorry, but if you do not want to do business there or if you can't compete against the Chinese, do something about it. Isn't this what we are told when we have a problem—crap or get off of the pot?

However, in a kick to the groin as per usual, when a leader complains, his or her complaint is considered dialogue or a sharing of ideas. But if you complain about these very people during a time when debate is most needed, you are labeled everything in the "not good book," aren't you? Did Bill Martyr really deserve to lose his show over the comments he made—because of sharing his opinions? I thought people were free. Listen, either you are with me or you are with the terrorists. Either you are a good employee or you are a complainer. Either you can follow the rules or you are an anarchist. When did I choose for my life to be decided by what someone else thought about me? Have you ever thought of that? When did you bestow upon society your life?

Those above you in the fictitious hierarchy of life complain all the time; we just don't get to hear it. But what is good for the goose is good for the gander, right? To be honest, though, I am not sure what a gander is, so hold one on second. Okay, they are both geese, so perfect! The idea that complaining is somehow bad vexes me, but who am I to have any opinion about this world? I am only renting my plot.

On the flip side, people who want to control you will say "stop complaining" if they are uncomfortable with where you are going with your speech or if they are too busy. But sharing an opinion is your right, doing so and isn't "bad"—even if it does make some people's blood boil. This blunt tool for killing freedom and controlling others can be used by all and not just the rich, but note that the "stop complaining" comment is usually used by people who are above you in some societal hierarchy way. Perhaps it is your boss, an elder, your parents, or just some bully who is trying to impose his or her will. Screw all of them!

In the end, complaining is just a way for a person to share an opinion about who he or she is and what her or she is thinking, and everyone has that right to express him or herself. So, unless you want to tell those who complain a lot to find a solution, get better or happier, and move on, let people be. Doing so is okay and, perhaps, may even be beneficial to the complainers—if the advice offered is good of course.

As an aside, it has been said that, if you consider someone a friend and you lie to him or her, you are, in fact, his or her enemy. So be honest. As a result, you may have to take the short-term pain—such as being yelled at, ostracized from a certain group, or kicked in the groin, but knowing the person will be better off in the future because you tried to help him or her makes everything else worthwhile in my books. Of course, I have never thought about what would happen if I was wrong, but ... Next!

Half Full or Half Empty

BEFORE WE MOVE ON, I want you to think about my choice to move on. Am I trying to get you to keep reading, thus, being "selfish" by moving on? Or was I genuinely thinking about you and being "kind?" Is doing what others want you to do a sign of having no "confidence"? Or does doing so show that you are "strong" enough to refrain from thinking that everything that happens in life is a battle that needs to be won? Are there answers to such questions? Are there always two sides to every story? I will let you decide this, as no one should be burdened with that duty other than you anyway.

Definition time:

Using labels: (1) a sign of laziness and ignorance; (2) life, so get over it, retard

---

As you may know, I have been feeling very robotic lately—like a robot with a shorted-out fuse I may add. But it is amazing what can happen to your life when you choose to believe in or focus on something different than what you are accustomed to. I feel like such a different person now. Really, I do. All I have to do now is pick up momentum and keep on rolling, like a rock rolling down a steep hill. Of course, a rock going down a hill gets chipped and actually gets smaller, so while I wish to lose weight. I am not sure this symbol for positive change is for me. On top of that, "going downhill" isn't generally associated with something positive.

Now, why did I have to say that? Am I a "negative" person? Is the glass half full or half empty? Or is there a situation-dependant gray area here, much the same as there is for everything else in life? We should examine this question, as being labeled according to your choice of terms-empty or full—is ridiculous. As in most situations in life, more than just two options exist. Let us begin the test.

Imagine you were in some desert surrounded by inedible lizards and poisonous cacti and, miraculously, came across a glass of water that was 50 percent full. Would you care that it was only halfway full? I don't think so. I imagine you would be pretty happy. But how about if you were in a restaurant that charged for water in this material world and ordered a glass of water that cost twenty bucks? What if the beaker came 50 percent empty? Would you be "positive" about this and see this glass as half full? I think that you probably wouldn't. It's more likely that you'd be looking for a way to get one of your hairs into your five hundred-dollar dinner so you could get your money back. And so you know, I am picturing that you are bald while I write this.

Why do I think this? Well, simply because life isn't a test that only has black or white results that can be easily categorized. We adore generalizing things we see into "knowledge" because doing so is easier than actually working to discover the truth. Cue the expert to come and tell me I am "depressed" and have low "self-esteem" because I think the glass is half empty. This is, sadly, what life has become—ambiguous options we call freedom but with only two possible outcomes; either you're in or you're out. Bite me, Doctor Frank-Einstein, as you may be wrong.

When I used to abstain from eating meat, on a tangent coming from left field in order to kill the time we have until we reach the gas station, people would ask me right away why I didn't or chide me for wearing leather, as if they knew I didn't eat meat because I was concerned about the welfare of animals. These people were trying to make me wrong or give me yet another label—hypocrite. I never said I couldn't or wouldn't eat meat; I simply chose not to. Buzzard off!

Just for fun, though, you should go online and do a search for "famous vegetarians." Did you know people like Edison, Newton, Socrates, Plato, Emerson, Einstein, Franklin, the Buddha, and many more great thinkers were all proponents of not eating meat? The smartest and brightest in our world all thought consuming animals in the name of health was bad for us. Interesting! Of course, many great athletes are and were also vegetarians, so the story we are told that we need to consume meat and dairy products to be strong appears to be false. Mike Tyson is a vegetarian—minus Holyfield's ear—as is super Olympic champion Carl Lewis. Add to that list Dave Scott, a five-time winner of the Ironman Triathlon. If anyone needs to be strong and full of energy, I would guess it would be him—interesting, to say the least. Many great thinkers and athletes, of course, are or were not vegetarians and eat/ate meat. But the vegetarians listed in this paragraph alone make up a pretty cool collection of people.

Of course, being a pleasure-seeking and stressed-out society, we need some outlets, right? I mean, take away movies, television, the Internet, porn, and sporting events for example, and we really do only have a few things left in life that can help us enjoy our boring days while we try to ignore our terminal stress. Those handful of simple items include foods such as ninety-nine different brands and flavors of chips, four thousand different types of candies, three hundred brands of chocolate bars, and a plethora of cookies; all kinds of gut-wrenching booze that makes people crazy; a never-ending array of mind-altering drugs; stress-relieving cigarettes; and many other great products that also kill us. So of course we are going to consume the flesh of dead animals and the fluids we squeeze out of them. We are only human, right? We really need more options available to us so we can enjoy our lives more. I have gone at the meat and dairy industry for a bit. For the record, though, I ate meat in my day. Back to not living by what you think is right.

Definition time:

Taste buds: only 25 percent of taste.

On a slightly different topic, we are told our whole lives that we can't or are not supposed to do certain things, aren't we? What happens when someone says to you that you can't do something? Most look at ways to get even or they try the forbidden fruit, right? If marijuana was legal but someone told you do not try it, you would most likely want to because we are a naturally curious species. But being told what, and what not to do, causes problems in our perfect little worlds. We get this sort of "over-parenting" our whole lives about so many different things that are at our fingertips, so naturally we need outlets that are more than just malls. We are human, and nothing can change that—not even a system based on norms, morals, tyrannical leaders who rain down upon us from every direction ideas we are supposed to live by, and on and on we go. We are oppressed in very many ways, so we need outlets to, ironically, keep life from imploding.

What if I said meat was bad for you but you can try it? Do you think you would? I bet most would. Many would think, *Cool, I am doing something that is bad*. And in a way, this makes people feel more alive. In cases like meat, we just enjoy without the guilt, don't we? Enjoying delicious food gives pleasure to the person, so for moment they think they are happy.

This is the worst kind of addiction, but for society—meaning the rich—this form of addiction is seen as okay because it is allowed and, of course, because it makes big business a great deal of cash. What a life. You use the government's accepted outlets your whole life, which is good for the system. But as a reward for being a good, little soldier, when you are older and develop a disease from living off of one or more of life's pleasures that are legal, you are forced to pay back all the money you made to pharmaceutical companies. Nice! Your socialization is a lie, people, so forget the outlets and find a better way. Most diseases today arise from stress and poor diets. If you need a number of outlets, maybe it is time to ask why.

So do you think it is possible for society to be doing this to us—slinging options that are bad for us because our morbid leaders understand this gives people the release they need and because providing that release keeps people in check-without our knowledge? Think about what happened when the American Government made alcohol illegal. There are sure a lot of things we are not supposed to do, but we also have a great number of outlets we can enjoy legally even though they are bad for us. We could be talking physical health here, as well as both monetary health and mental health. For example, meat or LSD—pick one. All of a sudden, meat looks more than practical, doesn't it? Put enough really dreadful choices in front of people, and the only partially bad starts to look good, really good, doesn't it. But are you happier because of the choices that are made available to you or more miserable because you can never get enough pleasure to sustain happiness? This is the question you should ask yourself here.

In conclusion, I know what I want to say here, but I am not sure it is coming out properly. How about this? Everything that pleasures us in our world is there for our use and consumption because our leaders think people will need those pleasures to offset our unhappiness. But that doesn't mean we need to use them. This argument may be a little too close to insanity for some, but if I was smarter and could write better, you would be popping acid and eating tofu before you knew it. I also know "meat versus acid" may not have been the best comparison. But do you think alcohol would have been better? Think about that.

As you probably know, I am not the Buddha here. I am not saying you should be doing anything other than what you are doing now. This is your life to do with as you please, and I respect you for you. You can be a gun-toting, whiskey-swilling, kidney steak tartar-eating, and radical right-leaning person, and we could still have fun together. I have no problem with who people are. I am just setting the table with arguments, whether right or wrong, to help you think about what it is you believe in. Proving me wrong or getting excited about starting something new are both great ways to feel more emboldened or energized, so I am putting forward what I am for a reason other than just trying to be right. Do you get me now? I told you a long time ago there is a method to my madness. This new freedom thing I am now enjoying is really changing me, for the record—like when I get a haircut.

Okay, so let's get off this gurney of death and enjoy the last fifty pages together. How about I just talk you through it; I am pretty disabled here, now.

THE GAS STATION EPISODE

I PULL INTO THE gas station one hundred pages later, amazed to see the pumped-up cost for liquid gold. Maybe there is a wheat shortage somewhere in the world, so the prices went up. This is crazy talk, but if coffee prices can go up because of a milk shortage, who knows what is possible. And that was true by the way. I did not make that up earlier. Coffee prices went up because of the demand on milk products and the corresponding rise in its price a few years ago. Weird, though, isn't more demand good? Doesn't it make the coffee industry more money? Nonetheless, the cesspool of fear has begun to whip up more ferociously just off shore and in close proximity to where all of the oil wells sit, boding evil.

And as an aside, thank you-let's call you, BeePee so I do not have to use footnotes—you degenerate, money hungry, and environment hating leader of our business world. One year after the worst oil spill in American history, you are making record profits again while still finding time to slap a $40 billion lawsuit on others, as if they were responsible for the huge mess you made-and cover up-you were caught participating in. What is wrong with this picture? Create a disaster by cutting safety standards, try to cover up the truth, change the CEO, and then say it wasn't your fault and sue what amounts to mom-and-pop businesses relative to BeePee for more money than you even had to pay out. Do I have my facts right here? Sigh! The way big biz tries to push everyone around makes me want to cry.

I read one report online stating BeePee did, in fact, try to steer the research away from the truth and toward a direction that would assist in making them look better. Internal e-mails exchanges in which top officials discussed ways to mislead the public were exposed. I am sure there are many articles online depicting BeePee executives as liars and so on, so as per usual look this up and see the truth. And the truth here I wish for you to seek is not that BeePee had a huge oil spill in the Gulf but rather, that companies and even countries will do whatever is necessary to mislead you.

And if what we read in the paper or hear on the news is a lie, what else is? Start questioning everything. Ask why we should live any differently than a huge company that does whatever it wants? Of course, huge companies pay a fine when they get caught committing a crime. Then make $6 billion dollars the following year. And if we try to cheat on our taxes or something like that, we go to jail.

We are always on public trial, but businesses can operate under the sick blanket of power, can't they? Our power gets cut, our heat turned off, our cars and houses taken away without mercy, and that is life. But when a company has a problem, what do we do? Do we hope everything will be okay as soon as possible because we think we need their services? Big business also means big power, doesn't it?

Of course, people who lead countries also use their power for personal gain, don't they? I afraid this happens more than we know. I am only assuming this to be true, as if I stated this as fact, I would be grouped with the conspiracy theorists and approached by those who like wearing running shoes and drinking Kool-Aid. No thanks!

However, the following story is definitely true; you can easily verify it by simply surfing the net. I gave the Vatican a lot heck for helping some Nazi war criminals escape from Germany after World War Two, but the Americans did the same—even though the United States and Jewish people are "best friends." I will keep this short.

The CIA, after World War Two, helped many Nazi scientists escape Germany. Why? The organization's leaders saw an opportunity to help their own cause, so immorally or not, people like Wernher von Brawn were basically smuggled into the

United States. This process of being Nazis to America was called "Operation Paper Clip."

Von Brawn worked for NASA and, to make a long story short, all of the UFOs that were seen just after the war were more than likely the result of American scientists trying out new German technology. "The Bell," Roswell, and Kenneth Arnold's famous first UFO sighting of "The Wing" were all connected to the United States government operating under the radar. Amazing stuff. And what else has happened that we don't know about? I am sure there is more. But again, welcome to the world you live in but know nothing about. But we do know about the Tuskegee Syphilis Experiment, radiation testing on citizens, medical apartheid, and the Manhattan Project don't we. This track record of intended cover-ups is hardly admirable.

The CIA has clandestine bases all over the world, but agents aren't interrogating people illegally of course; the CIA just really needs an underground base in Somalia for humanitarian reasons. Now the press is saying the CIA was working with Muammar Gaddafi? What is the government cooking up now? We have no idea! It is scary that we are paying for whatever the government is doing, though, isn't it.

Well, enough said governments and their unethical behaviors in general and back to the high gas prices that no "leader" has anything to do with unless you live in Russia. If I don't fill up now, I will be the lone participant in the uphill car pushing Olympic event later today, which would be an unappealing examination of my stamina I think. So what can I do other than grease the engine of life and feed the beast? Yes, I could ditch this wonderfully conceived marvel of technology and take the bus but … I need a car, truly. As much as I like sharing the bus with people I do not want to be around, I think I will stick to my car, thank you.

Thinking about the price of dead dinosaurs, if this is in fact where oil came from, it is amazing how the focus on one feature in our simple yet mentally complex world always seems painfully constant and that one thing is a cheap piece of cotton and linen better known to us as money. For the record, money will soon be made of polymer, a kind of plastic. At any rate, the price of dead trees with words on them is too much; the cost for the extracted remains of an ancient life that we use for fuel is too high; the price for genetically unneeded but mentally necessary comfort foods and beverages like coffee keeps going up; and the bills from purchasing devices that help to blind us from our miserable lives never ends. I really find it arduous to fathom that I am here on this object we call Earth to be so worried about money.

Yet, of course, I want to feel accepted and good, so I do nothing; although, how often does my phone ring now? By living right, I am getting paid off like a hooker does by a cop. I get to stay out of jail, I get screwed, I am poor, and that is about it. The dangling carrot that I have pursued my whole life like a starved horse with tapeworm is now being chased by someone else because I am done.

Are we freaking mad? It seems we are always doing something for the next step, which in my mind doesn't really allow us to enjoy the part we're on. We are always running from something and toward some phantom quasi ideal we are taught to think is right. But judging from the results of taking this path, I think we can conclude that it is quite an irrational quest, to say the least. This is sort of like letting kids who are not old enough to drive sail around the world by themselves. Many seem to know this, but we keep running, and the world keeps on spinning my head silly. If you disagree with me, that's okay. But watch people as a light is about to turn from walk to stop—how many of them run to "make the light" so they can save what, one minute? We have become so conditioned to run that running has become an innate human function, sadly. Not only do people run for the light, if they make it, they look so proud of themselves, like they have won something. I don't get that. Yeah, great job!

All of a sudden break down faster than a nuclear reactor in the desert with its core exposed. I act tough sometimes, but my feelings are so powerful right now.

"What the hell am I doing?"

I keep on crying … I just want to be happy. How can I possibly live with knowing this world is as fair as insider trading on Wall Street among billionaires?

Knock, knock, knock. The guy pumping my gas interrupts me and tells me that I owe him eight hundred dollars.

I really want to floor the gas pedal and crash into something and end it all. The rage and sadness that I am feeling now is unbearable and unstoppable. I can't take it anymore. I punch the gas violently, and you know what I mean. Every blood vessel in my body wants to explode through my pulsating red and purplish skin as I try to drive myself away from my problems.

Fuck everything! Fuck off! Aughhh!

Nothing happens. My full car is not running. It just ate, so I guess it needs an hour. Sigh! I pay the eight hundred like a once gleeful kid in a candy store paying for a fifty-pound rock and get the hell out of there.

This is really the time I hit rock bottom. I just couldn't take anything anymore.

Back to Reality, Like I Ever Left

LIFE SUCKS! NO, THE perception I have of this material world bites my ass and keeps drilling further after that. I cry again. I just want to be more levelheaded. Is that too much to ask? I am so up then so down. Does everything need to be such an internal battle with me? I can't even buy a candy bar without beating myself up.

Don't do it Jamie, it is bad for you…But it tastes good.

It will make you fat…But I will go to the gym, and run a little more than usual.

It will give you zits…I won't eat any other junk food for the rest of the week.

It is a waste of money…But I will only buy a small coffee tomorrow.

Do you really need it, Jamie…Of course I do not need it, but I want it.

Do you really want it or is it just a craving…A craving, but it is not going to kill me.

You will regret it after…But you will have joy for a few moments, and it is not that big of a deal.

Be strong, don't do it…Oh no, Jamie.

And then the guilt. Nice! The battle of the memes—a word coined by Richard Dawkins in 1974 but with origins dating back to 1844—rages on.

Anyhow, feeling like I do, I forego the much-needed grocery shopping and head straight for home. As I am driving home, I think about what just happened. I thought I was feeling so happy, but then all of a sudden, I was insanely manic-like Jack Nicklauson (play on the two famous men-Jack Nicklaus and Jack Nicholson) playing golf with a car windshield in the city. Maybe I need to go see a doctor? Maybe I am "clinically depressed" and need some drugs to help me cope with my thinking and this world?

Are pharmaceutical drugs really the answer to mental disorders that have been diagnosed by people who have merely been socialized to think differently than I have been? Are we being genetically modified in order to make us good little consumers? Or are some humanoids really in need of drugs if they appear depressed or socially different than others? And again, here, I am not talking about truly mentally ill people. I am more interested in those who merely think they are stressed-out, depressed, and so on. Perhaps Tom Muse can help us out on this one.

I wonder if something is really wrong with my genetic "makeup." (Interestingly, we use the same word for junk women put on their faces that merely transforms them in some small way into something or someone else as we do to describe who we truly are.) Or am I just seeing clearly what this world really is about and finding the truth depressing? Am I going or coming? I would just go smoke a joint, but that would be illegal and bad for me. I "know" smoking plants that are grown naturally in nature is bad for me. I was told so by many people when I was growing up. I guess it's better to go see a doctor and get a prescription for synthetic drugs that come in bottles with skulls on them and information labels warning me that what I am taking may have side effects such as nausea—which I already have from this world—constipation, and liver damage. Thanks for making me feel better, idiots!

Definition time:

Contemporary society: the deadliest virus of today's world.

Good night, everyone. Thanks for sharing this day with me. Although my day wasn't perfect, I am pretty happy with it. I know one thing for sure. I'm free and nothing is going to stop me from having the best sleep of my life tonight. See you at home, maybe.

I am running but something seems different this time. I peer over my right shoulder and into the eerie darkness knowing that objects could seem closer than they appear but there is nothing to see. As a gaze forward, the blackness of night; hold on, what light beyond yonder breaks the horizon? Is it the sun, the moon…Or my big break I have been waiting for?

To my surprise, it is none of those! I yank my steering wheel right, narrowly avoiding the oncoming traffic. Wow, that was close. Maybe I should be drinking and driving—coffee that is. Falling asleep at the wheel is scary. Weird how I wanted to hit the wall back at the gas station, but now I am, with "super person" like reflexes, doing what I can to save myself, though. There is nothing like having to appease two personalities. It has been said that it is easier to live one complete life than two half ones, but I am and was like my writing—everywhere.

I know I am jumping around and repeating topics here and there, but I would rather listen to a ten-minute story broken down to five two-minute slots busted up again over two hundred minutes than listen to one long story for ten minutes straight. See what I'm saying here. The minutes are the number of book pages. So while I talk about businesspeople over and over, I do so in small increments, so the subject stays fresh—like margarine on a kitchen table. If you did not get that, I will explain; margarine is like one or two molecules away from being a plastic. Not even bugs eat margarine that's left sitting out, as it is not really a fresh food—or any kind of food for that matter. The point here is I know I have spoken enough about businesspeople. The topic must be getting old. Well, we're almost done, so no harm, no foul—I hope.

Well, since I am now up and, in a way fortuitously, in front of the grocery store, I decide that I should pick up a few things. I pull in, park without incident, and head on in. You may as well just hand me the Pulitzer, now.

ROUND TWO
AT THE GROCERY STORE

TO MY DELIGHT, THE barnyard is relatively empty—much like the shelf where the pile of fresh fruit used to be. Brown bananas anyone? I love bananas, but not even a monkey would eat these ready to serve blended smoothies that come with a free side of fruit flies. Let's move on!

As I grab my desired items, I am struck by the similarities between life in a grocery store and life outside of this indoor zoo. Everything in here is itemized. We are forced to walk down narrow aisles. The many different choices of items we can purchase give the illusion of freedom. But think about it—we are stuck in a store while we exercise this freedom, and of course, the ultimate breadwinner, money, is important if you want to get what you think you need.

I am struck with the desire to do something crazy in here. Wouldn't it be fun to start a huge food fight now? Letting the full-sized kid out and having fun again seems like a great idea, but of course I do not do this. I did do this once years ago using Chinese food with my girlfriend at her stables. The end result was that we gave new meaning to the dish "chow mane." I can hear the moans from here.

Oh, look at this—a new product from Chile. This is interesting. You don't see many food items from Chile in here. I take everything back that I just said; life in here is awesome. I decide to buy the Chilean chili packet that was mixed in China with enough monosodium glutamate to give your unborn babies a headache and continue on down aisle twenty-four.

An activity I find interesting in grocery stores is watching people when there is food sampling going on. People who coincidently mosey by taste testing tables and then only sample one of whatever is trying to be sold makes me laugh; especially when they pretend to be interested in buying the product. But, of course, they do not purchase it. This is kind of like going to a restaurant and ordering Perrier when you really only wanted a glass of water. People all over the world always seem to be so fixated on what other people think of them. Wow, I am so sophisticated, and the waiter likes me, so yippee! As a former waiter and just so you know, we hated all people who drank just water—even if bottled. Drink wine, it is good for you—so I've heard.

This may seem a subtle observation and sampling a subject hardly worth mentioning. But for starters, how many of us really like eating just one of something? In this case of, I bet you *"can"* eat just one; we pretend to be polite and civilized by sampling only one small morsel from a container into which a thousand hands have reached before you (yummy). Some want more at that point, but they succumb to the social ideology that suggests that appearance is everything— and over a stupid free sample? I have rarely if ever seen someone go to town on a sampling table. This is pretty amazing. I may be way off on this, but tangents are my joy, so humor me for a bit.

Even though we've done the right thing and had only one sample, I think most of us really want to eat a few more soiled but free tasters without the guilt of worrying about what others may think or say. But because we feel self-conscious, we don't tempt fate. We don't indulge ourselves because social mannerisms, etiquette, and the essence of another label we have been force-fed to believe in yet oddly enough ferociously battle—"maturity"—come into play.

And of course, if you do eat too many samples, you'll be seen as a pig, right? Some people may label other's actions (like trying only one free sample) "good manners." But why? Why is this proper behavior? Do you get that? I don't. Where does it say we should only try one? Who decided that we mustn't try, God forbid, two? And what comes atop this scrumptious maturity cake in our teachings? A delectable layer of responsibility. This whim sounds so yummy I want to be cognitively bulimic. (I noticed that, in South Korea, people would eat more than one sample; some would even bring their own chopsticks.

With regard to sampling and being responsible, we choose to control our urges and impulse desires in favor of people seeing us as normal—whatever the hell that is. Keep this in mind; the moments we'll remember most when our lives are said and done are the ones during which we did something wild and "out of character" (OOC), as in those moments life lives forever. Is this not true? Do this right now. Think about some of the memories you have of your life. Aren't the ones that stick out the ones where you made yourself laugh or were just having a wonderful time?

I remember crazy things like passing out in front of my high school because I drank a bottle of Vodka much too quickly after playing floor hockey. That episode landed me in the hospital, where I woke up to my father's not-so-happy face. I also remember doing things I thought were embarrassing, such as looking like an idiot while singing and dancing to music while at a department store. I made others laugh as well, so I guess that's not a bad thing. I will never see those people again anyway, so who cares, right? But these are the times I remember so clearly now.

My mind is riddled with stories like these. My fondest memory may just well be the time I actually delivered a motivational seminar to a group of people. I held the seminar at the university I attended soon after I graduated. People were always looking to me for help, and I loved helping, so I thought this course of action was my destiny. I organized, wrote, preformed, and advertised for the seminar; I did everything in fact. I sucked because, as it turned out, I was not that happy. But at least I tried to overcome the number one fear in the world (public speaking) while at the same time helping others. I am proud of that. I never thought it was possible that businesspeople, police officers, students, and others would pay to hear me speak, but they did. Some were not even my friends.

As many others have said before, you never know what's possible until you've tried the impossible. I tried the improbable once. It was called trying to get *Purging Matters* published by the conservative folk who thought they knew better than me. But I showed them—my behind. They are on the way out because they did not mold themselves with the times, so self-publishing it is. Either that or I am just bitter.

This just in: A new study found that drinking coffee can help protect you from some cancers (prostate) but may bring on others (lung). The maybe doctrine is alive and well. Thank you, experts, you hermaphroditic schooled fishes.

What's next? Will we learn that milk is bad for our bones but good for keeping us strong? Really, if there is any question concerning things we eat that can possibly kill us, why not just get rid of those products from our world? Oh, yes, we are free and have the right to eat and consume things that kill us that, of course, have first been approved by one of our many government bureaucracies. Olestra, camel coloring, potassium bromate, and sulfites (and the list goes on and on) are all additives that have proven negative effects on our well-being. Yet they are in some of the foods we eat. We don't have to eat them. But, do I need to read every label to see if "zxygoklyzide" is in my food? Yes, I made that one up. If it is bad for me, get it the hell out of my food. The government has approved these and other additives but takes no responsibility for those who fall ill from them. Thanks. There is nothing like having to eat for your health while hoping you don't die from some non-genetic form of cancer.

This just in: experts are as helpful as coffee. The end!

Was I acting OOC when I was running a speaking seminar or getting drunk and passing out on the front lawn of my high school? What a strange thing it is for someone to say his or her actions were OOC. How can someone be OOC?" Why should we feel embarrassed if we make ourselves or others laugh by simply being ourselves? Who cares if we are seen as silly or "crazy?" Do not label your actions as OOC. Doing so will just suppress the life that lives within you.

Let's get back to the woman who is talking like this is about to happen now and is not just part of a bigger picture.

"Excuse me. Excuse me. Could you please help me?" The gentle request comes from a woman who looks pleasant enough and is wearing a bewildered look on her face.

"Sure," I reply.

I accept this writing award with great honor. I would like to thank my parents for fucking me up so much my intolerability for everything has become comedic relief to others. (As an aside but on the topic of awards, just once I would like to hear a real acceptance speech at some elegant red carpet show. Fuck you, you, you, and especially you! Thank you for this award, but fuck it as well! Of course no one would do this because it would mean the loss of his or her career. So these blowholes say what is right—at least until they drink a little too much.

"Do you know how to tell if a watermelon is good or bad," she asks sincerely?

Please, put your women products away I think as I look to see what else she is carrying. We humans are naturally curious, but sadly, this great gift dies as we age.

Crazily enough, I think I do know how to tell a bad watermelon from a good one, so I respond, "Yes I do."

I can hardly contain myself now as this writing is beyond parallel of any of the greats that came before me.

Yes, I agree, there is room for "responsible chatter" in this world. I shall try to refrain from such thoughts of grandeur. I was just trying to have fun, though, so don't make me cry. Fasten your seat belts people, as we are now going for a guilt trip.

"All you have to do is knock on it like this," I tell her (*tap, tap,*

tap). "And if it sounds somewhat hollow, then it should be okay. Also, I think, this should be small," I add, pointing toward, and forgive my French, the butt of the watermelon.

"Thank you," she replies with a smile as I walk away.

"You're welcome," I say, directing a little wink her way while thinking what a nice woman she seemed to be.

I said she seemed nice because, of course, even though we had a nice encounter, I still do not really know her. Anyway, right after this happened, a strange feeling came over me. I felt a bout of silliness possess my lifeless body. I was going to do something OOC now. I actually started to knock on the guavas as if they were watermelons.

I had no reason to be playing the bongos with guavas, but at that same moment, the watermelon woman walked by and asked, "What are you doing?"

"I really have no idea," I responded.

We both stopped dead in our tracks with quizzical, yet happy looks on our faces and then burst out laughing. What a moment. These are the times you remember I think when your life is just about over, and I am talking from experience here.

Thinking back, I can remember many such encounters when I did something a little off the wall and received the best response back. One moment that still makes me cry today (even as I type this) happened many years ago. Back in 1998 when I was in Cuba and staying at the Beaches Resort on Veradero Beach, I was eating dinner alone in one of the beach's many restaurants when a magical moment occurred for me. The person that was taking care of me that evening had seemed a little sad the whole night, so when I received my dessert, I turned the cake into a heart and then handed it back to her. She saw this and almost started to weep. She had to literally bite her lip to stop herself from crying. The presentation, the heart, the smile, and the warmness with which I treated her touched something deep within her, and in a Newton theory type of way, the response did the same back to me. This story may seem small and insignificant with regard to the grandness of it all, but sometimes that is all it takes to create a long and lasting positive memory—showing someone that you care in the simplest of ways. In this case, believe it or not, it really was a magical moment that I will cherish forever. I cry every time I read this. Oh, and as an aside, Cuba is beautiful, and the people are incredible.

Isn't it remarkable how simple gestures seem to provide people with a great deal of warmth? Even small drops of water, if continual, can fill a tub, just like small tokens of love can fill a heart. With regard to love and compassion, why is it that we take these two wonderful and most needed human qualities for granted until the last moments of our lives, or sadly, when it is too late? What time is it?

During the course of a human's life—and course is a good pun, as it does feel like we're constantly being schooled or scolded by our teacher, and society-loving inhabitants are continuously forgiving others—in public anyway—but most never seem to give themselves a break. People say it is okay, for whatever someone may have done, but then go home and tell a story of how rude this guy was today, as an example of receiving a public apology. Why some people are so hard on themselves, yet, "light" with others is beyond me. You are as deserving of respect, love, and appreciation as anyone. So don't forget to give yourself some credit, a break, or whatever you need because, in a thankless world, there may not be always people around to do that for you. And yes, a tree in the forest does make a sound when it falls even if there isn't anyone around to hear it. That is as loving as I can get, by the way. My little moment down memory lane connected me with my softer side, but I am back now and ready to kick some verbal ass! It is too bad I never let soft Jamie out. Things could have been much different if I had.

I finish my shopping, pay, and then head for home leisurely. Even though I am hard on myself, I do feel that I had a good day—minus the gas station episode. That part was a little disheartening, but there's nothing I can do about that now.

Why do I want to cry again? I am happy! I am happy! I am happy! I will have to see you at home.

I add a little more food to Babo's food dish and then, without delay head directly to bed. What a day. Being unemployed is hard work and stressful. Good night!

My Last Dream

I AM RUNNING. I am sprinting away from the life I have been taught to believe is real toward a life I have no idea about. There is no mistaking both paths are one in the same, but I keep on mentally racing away, anyway. The world I see is painful, so around and around I go.

The running—or the appearance of it—away from my life is a time-tested scientific method of trying to avoid my thoughts and nothing more. Of course, there is nowhere to run, as everywhere I go, there I am. This system is as clever as … Well, it is really not that intelligent at all.

What would happen if I stopped fleeing and actually questioned myself regarding what I thought I knew? What would truly be the consequence of such "perverse" action? Would I die? Would some disease, perhaps mental, devour my already lifeless body? I could lose my job, if I had one to lose, but that's not too bad a consequence, as I can always get another one. Losing a job is better than forgetting my principles, my mind, and my heart; that's for sure.

Today feels different, though. I am tired and don't feel like running now. What is happening to me? I stop dead in my tracks; I am unable to move. This is the last stand of Fear Blown Apart. I am awakening and ready for whatever comes my way. The infant light of life that has always lived within me begins to shine brighter, like that of a lighthouse light during the day. The epic struggle for freedom rages on flat-footed and mindfully obtuse.

I am almost there I think, but a thick fog begins to blind me from the light. Even in the moment of enlightenment, I am lost. *Keep digging, Jamie. Stay the course, Jamie. You can do it! Ironically, stop the running and get to where it is you want to go. Be strong! You are almost there*-I am almost there. Five, four, three, two, one...

Symbolically, the song, *Sunglasses at Night* is playing on the radio.

BANG!

What the heck is going on? You have to be kidding me. I have no idea why my alarm was set, as I have nothing planned for today. But Coronary Heart? (Corey Hart for those who did not get that joke or recognize his famous song, *I wear my sunglasses at night*.) Maybe Megadeth, I could understand. Wow! What a way to start the day! Enough said—for this page, anyway!

Weirdly, as I said that I had a vision of Bob running by my room. That is all I need now. Anyway, excuse me.

/AVING TIME

SINCE I HAVE NOTHING planned for today, making a positive out of something brutal only one page later, I guess I can choose to lie here without worrying about being late for work, or I can sleep in stress free if I wish. I must admit, though, I do feel a little uncomfortable about having nothing planned. Oops! Well, at least the stress machine is up and running. Back to reality—that quickly!

Excuse me, please. Nature is calling. But, interesting, is this trip to the bathroom nature or nurture? If I hadn't had those couple of drinks last night, would I have to be going to the bathroom now? In a grander scale, does nurture cause nature to be as we see it? Or is our one, big, unhappy family nature's mystery? Nature or nurture—you can fiddle, but it will always be a riddle!

After a lovely pee that felt naturally pleasing, I continue on with the morning ritual, even though my life has turned upside down. I am a creature of habit. After a shower and breakfast, which consisted of two grapefruits and a bowl of oatmeal with raisins, I shoot out the door with my keys in hand.

I decide almost without thought to head back to the bookstore. I have nothing else to do, so I figure this bearing is the best course of action. Maybe I'll try to get a job at the bookstore while I'm there. I could read for free while making a buck—literally. I once had a job that enabled me to listen to books on tape while I worked, and I loved that. I was only twenty at the time, but still, I should look into this. Of course I won't because I wouldn't be able to make enough money to buy my dream, but it was a nice thought.

As I am walking to the bookstore, I notice a man sitting in his vehicle. He is waving his arms wildly like a crazed octopus, while honking his horn like a sunglasses-wearing rapper would while interrupting an acceptance speech—arrogantly and pathetically. Can you really honk a horn? Or does the horn make a sound when the required apparatus is pushed? If the latter is true, is it logically correct to say a man was in his car honking a horn? I ask myself questions like this all the time for some reason. Sigh! The inconsequential battles in my mind rage on continuously like a fight between my multiple personalities—insidiously.

Back to the old man frolicking about in his car like a squid traffic cop giving directions to oncoming motorists and to the angry jellyfish-like woman who is stuck behind him, while we're at it. I am thinking that I used to be one of these funny, little creatures—in a mental panic but with nowhere really imperative to get to. And when I say *imperative*, that excludes racing off to the store to buy some snacks and then rushing back home to watch *American Idol*. Priorities, people!

As an aside, I have a great idea for a reality television show. Hold on there; give me a chance. Yes, my show would be set on the edge of what is deemed suitable in our crazy world, but I think my idea is not only bold, it is smart; it would show the human side to suffering in a positive light. My proposal is this: Let's round up a group of drug addicts, (Sorry but I do not know the politically-correct name for this group of people. Maybe, straight or sober challenged?) require them to get straight, and then have them compete for a life-changing job like the one available to the contestants on *The Apprentice*. It would be harsh but also warm in ways we cannot even imagine now. Let's face it; this program would be more entertaining than watching some lame ass reality show about some "pretty" person, whose idea of morality is a three-week marriage, a sex tape, and a great deal of drama for no other reason than having no talent to do anything else.

Wouldn't my reality show be fun to watch? Not only would you get to, presumably, see a great deal of questionable behavior from the comfort of your living room, you also would get to witness people who most of us have no more contact with than to walk over them on the way to work, try to overcome personal problems. I believe people would warm up to these contestants and the show would be a huge success. If some guy can become a web hit because of his voice, imagine what could happen here. I would call my show *On Cloud Nine*. Am I wrong? Anyway, think about it, executives.

Now, getting back to the invertebrates who are dancing about in their cars like chopped-off tentacles in a warm skillet, as I declared earlier, the majority of people usually think what they're doing is of the utmost importance; but really what is imperative to one person is only trivial to another. My cousin, Tom, used to laugh (maybe he still does, but I have not seen him in quite a while) at people who tried to drive around like Formula One drivers. He'd ask, "Why do these people want to rush to the next red light?" Unless you plan on running lights all the way to where you are going, like I did in South Korea (when in Rome), then there is no point speeding past people just to save two seconds, is there? We all try to save time here and there, but has anyone ever really added up this "saved time." If not, then why bother. Some may save money, but do any of us really save time?

What are the consequences if you don't get to a place as quickly as you can? Do you think that, unless you're following the traffic laws and bulldozing your way to the mall, you're wasting your time? Do you really think it's a waste of time to sit in traffic or behind an elderly lady who can barely see over the dashboard—a perilous situation attributed to an all-too-common but preventable case of osteoporosis? I AGREE! Fly, man, fly! Forget waiting if you don't want to. A red light is just a suggestion anyway.

As for red lights, can there be any more of them? I seem to get stopped at every second side street. City planners, if they can be called that, sure seem to have dropped the ball on this one. Cities are growing outwards and that can't be stopped, but as they do, the new housing areas, of course, require roads. At the end of each road, there is then a new light. Now, because of this, the main strip has turned into just a drag to drive.

Near my parent's place, which is in the country, much of the once vacant land that housed animals such as deer was developed for housing huge warehouses. Toyota, for example, actually received a large chunk of land for free-and the worker's wages paid for by the local taxpayers-just so the auto giant would plant themselves there. Other communities were also trying to lure Toyota to build within their land. Anyway, Toyota set up shop and twenty new, stupid lights were put in because of the plant. It must be nice to have that sort of drawing power. The rich get richer in yet another way, and the rest of us get more red lights to ignore. I can get a small business loan but that is about it.

On the flip side, if you drive erratically-like a wide eyed maniac who forgot to take his safe and synthetic medicine for the societal disorder he was afflicted with because he lives in a society that is mad—just to save time, the stress that comes with this sort of maneuvering may knock off years from your life counting back from the middle. So, it may be wise to invest in time now so you can have more to enjoy later, but that's up to you. There was a different sentence here, but my editor said I should take it out. So, these three are here instead. She obviously does not understand me.

Are you in a race? If you do think you're in a competition, against whom or what are you racing—time? Guess what, time—whatever time is—will always win, as it never goes faster or slower (unless you are in a time machine, I guess). The clock of life just keeps on ticking away no matter what we do, so if you are trying to save your time but are not spending it being in the moment, then in fact you are royally wasting it.

For example, if you saved ten minutes by speeding or breaking a few traffic laws but it still took you twenty minutes to get where you wanted to go, then, because you were so focused on saving time, you lost the twenty minutes due to being stressed-out and not really enjoying yourself. Your passenger may not be all that happy either, which makes the "saving" of time questionable. The ten minutes of arguing after is surely a waste of time, right? If you are playing out scenes from the movie *Crash* you may be doing all right, but how many of us are doing that? In the past I rushed everywhere; a lot of good that did me.

If you can drive fast and still find the time to enjoy the sights, then bravo! Personally, I used to drive like a maniac. But it was not my fault; society taught me to be like this. Anyway, I think it is safe to conclude that the jury is still deliberating on whether speeding is good or not.

A study about speeding concluded that, for people who like to drive fast, motoring along at a speed they feel comfortable with is safer for them. I guess when people who prefer "speeding" are forced to drive slow, they lose focus, become bored, and get into accidents more. I am only talking about citizens who in fact feel more comfortable driving fast—people like me for the record. And no, I did not fund this study, but it's good that you asked.

Of course, rushing around is part of our socialized mind—we cannot "waste time," as we need to "hurry up" and be "productive." Then, as your reward for being a good foot soldier, when it comes time for retirement, you can freely stop and smell the dressed-up and pretty dandelions for the 10 percent of the life you have left. No thanks. My life is mine to do with as I please. So sorry, you can't have my time, you green-eating goblins.

THE ART OF PROCRASTINATION

I SURE WALK SLOWLY, don't I? I guess I should hurry up. Procrastination takes on so many forms it's hard to stay focused and know when good quality downtime is just that and not time where we are "supposed" to be doing something else. But what is the act of procrastination? You guessed it—nothing. The word *procrastination* is just another dumb label; it's intended to make you feel you "should" be doing something more productive than whatever you found important enough to be doing whenever someone threw the label at you. The idea of procrastination is another seed long ago planted seed, a weedy idea grown by your guilty conscious. But how does this patch of death grow? How does society or someone cultivate this plot of mental land?

Of course, everything starts with your thinking, whether you want to admit this or not. But why do people think they should be doing something other than what they are already doing? For starters, while growing up, we are constantly told what our priorities should be, and naturally, these suggestions become part of what we believe in and value. But as we get older, these very same ideas that once took precedence over everything else may change for some of us, and this is where our brains become confused. Even though our priorities have changed, ours brain haven't forgotten what we've been taught we should be doing—what's right—so an internal battle ensues. This is where the idea you are procrastination comes from. You may think you want to be chilling out, but another region of your brain is simultaneously saying otherwise. I never worried about "vegging" out when I was younger.

It's hard to forget what you already know, isn't it? Try to convince someone who has been educated via any religion that what he or she believes in is wrong and see what happens. Every part of your socialization works the same way as well. Some people may become less or more strict regarding their religious beliefs once they are older, but getting those basic lessons from youth—whatever they may be—out of your mind is impossible, isn't it? As an aside, I wish I could forget some of things I did when I was younger, but that is a story for another book.

As for the seed of "procrastination," let's look at an example. Consider the common phrase, "I should do the laundry." Laundry is a "necessary chore" one has to do at some point, but who says when you have to do it? Nowhere does it say that we have to do the laundry when the basket is full. But our whole world is structured around these "must do" activities. Some tasks, of course, we should do, but most societal duties are optional at best. How did we become such followers? The answer is a combination of *how* we learn—by association—and, of course, *what* we, in fact, have learned.

Throughout our entire adolescent lives, we watched someone, in most cases our mothers, do the laundry once or twice a week, and from this we learned that when the laundry basket is full, we "should" do the laundry. Now, every time we see a full basket of laundry, we feel like we "should" wash it. But this is just what our mother thought; it's what she believed was best for her. Universalize this thought while thinking about everything I have spoken about. You will see that a whole lot in our life works in this manner—whether right, wrong, or even unnecessary. We let life suck out reactions from us more than we respond to them. Most people just act without really thinking or knowing why.

I am now in front of the bookstore. Let's head on in. I will pick up where we left off here, in there. While there may not be a big difference between the two, I'm too tired to keep on fighting the losing battle. Only twenty or so pages to go; I am sure I can make it but we need to hurry.

CROOKED IDEAS

One technique I've used extensively to change the effects of the "nocebo" pill I was given to those of one that works like a placebo is to transform in my mind what things mean to me. For example, think of procrastination as a form of meditation if you have to. At least this is a positive activity to engage in—to some anyway. You can't please everyone all of the time because every person is the accumulation of thousands before him or her, so stop the "shoulding" and "self-berating" you may be giving to yourself and do whatever you want.

Anyway, I "should" get reading now. I grab the *D-Day* book, but before I get into reading, I prolong the period of feeling immensely and innately inadequate by scanning through the pages and cleverly decide that just looking smart is better than being wise. I am now meditating—works every time—as I look around frantically for someone to save me!

As I unemotionally peruse the words of wisdom printed in *D-Day*, I realize I "know" most of what is being said in here. Sadly, much of the information that I have read in these types of self-help books seem grounded in manipulating, which is, ironically, what has happened to some of the information in them as well. The information has been stolen and transformed to sound like something different. For example, hundreds of years ago the Philosopher, Aristotle, developed theories about how items like knives and forks became associated as one in our brains- an activity he called "the association of similarity, contrast and contiguity in time and space." Now, others have named this normal mental activity all kinds of fancy names in the guise of newfound knowledge and then have marketed it via publishers, television shows, and so on as such, but no, the idea is as ancient as this font.

Poor Aristotle can never catch a break. He *was* finally forgiven by the Catholic Church back in the year 2000 for having the audacity to claim that the sun was at the center of the universe and not the Earth, so good for him. Or was that Galileo Galilei? One second please... Galileo made the public statement in his work that the sun was at the center of the universe, but this after Copernicus almost a hundred years earlier had the idea that this was true. Copernicus wrote a book about this, but did not publish it. Pretty smart! Bill Martyr should have taken some lessons from him.

As an aside, just for saying the sun was at the center of the universe, Galileo was found guilty in court of heresy and was placed under house arrest for the remainder of his life. Sounds familiar today—say something wrong and, oh boy, watch out! The Church sure can roll with change, can't it? Think about that. And these astronomers were talking about the center of the universe, as back then, no one knew of solar systems and galaxies. Edwin Hubble, as in the Hubble telescope, announced in the 1920s that the sun was part of a galaxy and there were millions of these. Imagine if someone had suggested this back in the 1500s.

I wonder what else we will discover we were wrong about. Maybe the Church will be apologizing years from now to those who believe in abortion, euthanasia, gay marriages, cloning, and so on these days? The Church seems pretty good with going with the flow—after realizing of course that they have no choice but to accept whatever seems to be likely, popular, or "God" forbid, the truth; failing to do so means risking being seen as an afterthought. At any rate, life means change, so better late than ever with that apology.

I know you know the apologies I suggested won't happen, but the Earth and Sun thing is kind of big, so maybe, just maybe the Church will one day accept other notions it currently holds "contemptible"-not that people needs the approval from some Church. I am just saying that anything is possible. Look at me; it took me a whole page just to make my morning seem positive, but I did it, so who knows, stranger things have happened. Oh, I have been saying "the Church" a great deal, but of course I mean the Catholic Church. It is the predominant religion in the West, and I do not have the time to go microanalysis of all the religions out there, so mainstream it is. Sorry!

Getting back to the ideas of today's "great thinkers," some might have built up concepts that are more advanced, but never do I read mention of Aristotle when I read about concepts based on the foundation he laid, such as neuro-associative conditioning (NAC). I guess when people make themselves look smarter than they really are, they are better able to market themselves and, thus, make more money. Is that too cynical? Perhaps people who do try to help others have their heart in the right place, and the money is not important. But to me it still seems more about making money, as some cannot even give credit where credit is due.

And it's not just people trying to make money who misplace credit, of course; politicians work this angle all the time. That Pallid woman, when it came to the death of "Been Laid Out," thanked Bush for getting him but not Obama? Are you that insecure? Sadly, some people find this person energizing. She is not the role model for me; nor is her family for that matter. But oh well; you can't always be right, people.

Also, how can a twenty-year old single mother can be so important and interesting that she can have her own reality television show and a book out about her memoirs is stunning. I am talking about Pallid's daughter, here. Welcome to the new world, where the end product smells because bullshit sells. Really, people, you need to be stronger and not allow yourself to get sucked into this circus of stupidity. Pick up a hobby or something. But turn the television off and make these "reality" television mockeries of humanity get a real job.

This just in: Palin's movie was a bomb at the box office. This is news to me because I didn't even know she was in one. Anyway, please end like Seinfeld predicted would happen for those with no talent—by getting spit out of the bottom of the porn industry and going away. I can see it now—*Bear Buck does some Backdoor Camping with Alaska Wild.*

Being curious and getting back to bin Laden, was he even alive when the SEAL team killed him? Or was his death just a huge hoax? Instead of proving his death to the world, the United States government decides to send his carcass to the bottom of the ocean before anyone can see the remains? He killed people from other countries too, so what gave the United States government the right to do whatever they wanted with a cadaver that did not belong to them?

Some people claim that bin Laden's death was a hoax, of course. In any case, I found it amusing that some news agencies reported that he had a stash of porn in his home and that he told his family to go live in peace in the West. We are more similar than most people realize. I'm being insensitive, I know; but really, it was just a shot at Been-Laid-Out more than anything. Bin Laden tried so hard to appear like he was some hero but there he was… well, you know. What a symbol for hatred of the West he was—a guy living in a mansion who is reading porn. That is so not like us Westerners at all.

I will retract the statement about us being similar to bin Laden and say, instead, that he was evil, as clearly he was. My bad! But was Bin Laden part of some larger CIA operation as some say he was? Maybe I am apologizing too soon. What do we really know about what was happening behind the scenes? Like I pointed out earlier, current reports suggest the CIA was working with Gaddafi's regime. We know what we have been told. But would the CIA really come out and tell people that Osama really worked for the agency at one point? They already have told us they do not have bases in Somalia, Yemen, Poland, and the list goes on and on. I guess that when you're predominately an undercover agency telling people where you plan on setting up shop is not the way to go.

Look into things and ask questions about the events you see, read, and even believe now. You do not need to be rich to be knowledgeable. Knowledge may not bring you wealth, but it could make you more informed and thus happier. Where are your parents from? Who socialized them and in which country did that happen? What is normal in that country? Where did the concepts that founded that culture come from?

For example, do you know the history of marriage? It is not all that romantic to be sure. You may be surprised, or perhaps not, as you still see the entrails of the historical philosophy embedded in our system. The original purpose of marriage was not rooted in uniting people who were in love; instead, it was about money and possessions. Look that up for yourselves if you want to find out more. The answers for all of us, no matter where we are, are written in history.

Considering that the concept of marriage was founded upon money and inheritance and not family, one wonders why gay people aren't allowed to be tying the noose around their necks. If we are all equal, the homosexual community should also be able to feel the pain of wedlock—key word being *lock*. Seriously, we know the argument against legalizing gay marriages. But when you learn about the history of marriage and realize it had nothing to do with "God," what was written in the Bible, or anything about what is morally right—almost the opposite of morally proper, actually—you will see there is no good reason gays should not be able to get hitched. You may think there are reasons, but we have already talked about "knowing the truth," and the truth can be wrong, so let's move on. And to reiterate what I said earlier, New York and Washington State have now both passed a law allowing gay marriages, so times are changing.

Publishers—You Suck

WHAT WERE WE TALKING about? How about trying to get a book published? If you are already known or get backed by a large publisher, it is easier to get circulated and be successful, as your name or the publisher's label sells itself—or at the very least helps a great deal. If you are like me and have never published anything, getting your work printed and distributed by someone—even if what you have written is freaking amazing, ultra slick, and super intelligent—is almost impossible. This mental way of life—following what you think you know like one of Pavlov's dogs, is what I have been alluding to throughout the whole book—the system limits possibility. To be a writer, a successful one, publishers or agents want to see other work or credentials, as it makes their work easier and the potential for a greater bottom line more possible. This is even true when what is being repackaged and resold is just a collection of redundant and recycled ideas. I never wanted to write a book anyway, so all good here.

Why can't your dream be a reality and not just a nightmare? Harry Potter was just a dream for an unemployed woman on social assistance, but now look at her. These days, J. K. Rowling walks and talks like she was born of money. But to be sure, she is still that same old person just presented in a different light.

As an aside, I do have many other book ideas. So if you don't like this one, please let me know and I will fly some of my other ideas by you. One is a children's book called, *Shut the Frig up, Baby*, and my other book, about living with the elderly, will be entitled *Hurry Up, Geritol Man!* They will both be great like this one.

Aristotle isn't the only great thinker of the past whose ideas have been ripped off by authors using this "grafting" technique and their name to resell old ideas. For example, the idea that we see ourselves as reflections of how others see us was marketed as a great new and provocative way of thinking a few years back, but the idea has been around for a long time. Charles Cooley (whose name I mentioned earlier) devised the term *looking-glass self* over a hundred years ago; the idea was that we see ourselves as interpretations of how we think others see us. Yet, none of these "New Age" authors mention Dr. Cooley; rather, they use this idea as their own.

Dr. Cooley said that we imagine how we must appear to others; we imagine the judgment of that appearance; and we develop our selves through these judgments. Sound familiar to you? It was in another "top selling" book. Sigh! I think it was Mark Twain who said, "The ancients have stolen all of the best ideas." It is now time to write my eulogy.

All motivational type folks use wisdom from the past to highlight who they wish people to see them as, so doing so is, sadly, nothing special, sadly. Twain, unlike most of these folks, cleverly noted that that was the case. (I recently chuckled when I found a book filled with well-known Twain quotes being sold online by some other author). Many self-help gurus use old Buddhist sayings, religious teachings, and ideas from those long dead and buried as the foundation for their systems to make people feel better, but I wish that people gave credit to those who deserve it. Thanks…I will have to get back to you on that one.

Nowadays we are so conditioned to listen to those in "authority figures" because we have been told we should via our education that we, sadly, keep on doing just this. The fear of what we do not know makes us follow what we are told. But PhD or some other label attached to someone's name doesn't make him or her untouchable or worthy of unquestioned praise. Don't hide behind labels; stand by what you have said, my friend. And if what you have stated isn't yours, why not say so?

Publishers, quit trolling used ideas past people in order to make a buck. Have a little integrity here, you greedy moles. Of course it's possible that these self-help promoters have given credit to the thinkers that came before them and I am just ignorant.

If I am mistaken about this or anything else I have shared with you for that matter, I take full responsibility, as even though I have the right to think what I want, I don't want to share things with you that are not true. Do you believe that? You may want to rethink that viewpoint and read the book again while doing a little research on the side. Maybe, just maybe I have been telling you lies or bent truths just to teach you this very lesson. But in the end, what you want to believe is solely up to you. I know; I am not that nice. But remember that I said I'd take the short-term pain now, as later I know you will be thanking me.

Every time someone speaks, you are being sold something for reasons you may or may not know. If it's a medical doctor who's speaking, one would hope you are being offered the truth. But ask questions anyway and remember, if there is doubt, there is no doubt. Many people use their labels to sell you stuff for personal reasons—sadly, usually money. Do you want to buy a great book?

The big question you should ask yourself now is, "Do I want to be the seller or a buyer in this world?" Most of us are buyers of course because of how society has been set up and due to the fact most are not born into super affluent, game-creating families. All consumers need to make mindful choices, and doing so requires knowledge, not thoughtless reactions based on impulses. I am hoping this is part of that helpful information that one requires— even if I never listen to myself. I am against people using their positions to better their own, even more so when this shit kicking is at the expense of people like you or I. So, before you do anything from now on, be fearless, do your homework, and ask away.

As for "experts," you know I am not an expert in any field worth mentioning here, but I do worry about coming off looking arrogant because I always choose to use my mind and to speak candidly. *Outspoken* was another word I could have used there, but sticking up for yourself, asking questions, or disagreeing with people verbally isn't being outspoken, is it? This sounds like it is bad or something. To me, questioning people seems smart, but so sure does get nasty responses, doesn't it?

As for looking arrogant, if you knew my heart, you would know how warm I am and how I really just want to help others be happy—while avoiding looking into the mirror. I just can't seem to show who I am all of the time. Do you know what I mean? I have always had this huge wall that surrounds me, and without looking or knowing, I just verbally hurl whatever I can onto the people on the other side of the "burrow wall" to protect myself. I know every human walking the face of the Earth today has "insecurities" for one reason or another. But I have always been sensitive, so I was offensive because I was extremely defensive.

It's weird that I always felt this way, though, as many of my friends thought I was the most confident person they knew. Can I be as they see me unknowingly? What does it mean to be confident? What is being confident relative to—how people feel compared to what they think they see in other people (usually people they are envious of for some reason no less)?

This line of thinking is terrible for the psyche of course, as we're focusing, in one way or another (consciously or subconsciously), on our insecurities to begin this horrifying experiment with. Participating in this sort of thinking and action makes no sense because, like we do with everything else, we are using ignorant perceptions of the world to guide our boat—usually right into the welcoming rocks. Yet, sadly, I think most of us engage in just this sort of self-induced quagmire. Where is that damn lighthouse?

People are to us now what stars were to sailors back in the old days, like a million years ago—guides. However, think about this; all people are different, yet we still like to think we know what is going on based purely on observations. And of course you should realize that sailors primarily used one star—the North Star, not six billion of them. Think about that.

As for the notion of confidence, this pseudo character trait really only exists in the mind's eye. How do you know you are or are not confident and others are more or less so? Hook up the concepts of confidence with self-esteem, cast them off to the fish out there looking for anything to bite into, and see if you catch any groupers other than those hanging on to hope. I wish I was more confident or had higher self-esteem; yank, sucker fish on! Do not fall for this bait. You are fine; the system is messed up and you just don't have the right information; luckily, though, that can easily be rectified.

And just because someone chooses not to go out on the dance floor and get jiggy with it, does not mean he or she lacks confidence. If someone does this, it could very easily mean he or she just doesn't want to dance. I know I would not want to go to a karaoke bar. Surely that has nothing to do with whether or not I'm confident. Maybe it's a reflection of good taste. But think about thus; if everyone was dancing and only you weren't, I would think that you're extremely confident, as to be a "wallflower" and to stand out like a "sore thumb" takes more "confidence" than just trying to be like everyone else. That is truly impressive, my friends.

D-Day Revisited

LET'S GET STARTED ON the reading, shall we? I open up *D-Day* to the table of contents and scan the obituary section. Oops, wrong article of reading. I hope this is not an omen of things to come. I pick up *D-Day* and go through the process again, looking at the table of contents. I am looking for something that I think could help me feel better, now. Short-term gain, long-term pain is the unconscious motto of my world today. Pass me another Band-Aid please; no wait, call the cardiologist because it's time.

Well, that was getting a little too into "it" for me, meaning, it was hitting too close to home. As for what I read, well, it was interesting and a little different than other books that I have read. But for the most part, I obviously "knew" most of what the author was saying. Of course, I don't practice much of what I think I know because I feel I'm right to complain about the injustices I see all around me. So the question right now must be, if I already knew what I just read, then what is the problem? What was my problem? Why can't I beat my fear—the inbred cesspool of anxiety borne from my mind? Why am I so sensitive and afraid to be me?

I do wish, for the record, that I could have adhered to and understood the importance of the following three expressions:

1. Practice makes perfect,
2. Out of sight, out of mind, and
3. You get what you focus on.

I never practiced becoming a better person, and I was not conscious of how just knowing something meant I was not always aware of it; as a result, my focus was way off. What a sad life.

"The Power of Sleep" is next in the "kill them all" book, but I am too tired to continue on reading. Actually, to be honest, I am just tired of this kind of literary mumbo jumbo. I decide to put the book down and do what comes naturally, which is to think about nothing.

After relaxing in a rock hard, brown armchair for a few minutes and dreaming about being a superhero, I decide to pursue the information that has been printed in the conservative agenda— better known as the "newspaper." I need a job eventually, you know. As much as I like being free of work, how can I breathe without money? I would like to not have to work, but who wouldn't?

I think I was definitely born into the wrong era. Perhaps if I were to have been born during the time when single-celled organisms ran free, that would have been better; although, even then I lose, as I'm sure they didn't run.

THE NOOSE PAPER

WOW, THESE JOBS SUCK! Most are call center positions and/ or sales jobs that require you to work on commission only. Here's one I'm qualified for—a human scarecrow position is opening up. (I actually did this once just after university.) Airports and other places where people don't want birds hanging out or nesting call companies who specialize in bird scaring. These companies supply the grounds with bigger birds, like eagles, and people to help keep away the flying misfits. It was one of the easiest and best jobs ever. I tanned all day.

You need two years of experience and a master's degree to fill the position now, and I only have six weeks of experience and a BA that's not worth the paper it's printed on in an unrelated field. Damn!

Seriously, the jobs in here today all seem to require both nineteen degrees and forty years of experience. How does one get a job if he or she isn't even able to gain experience? And then there are the bunch of ads in here looking for prostitutes—those willing to go out and sell themselves and some product for the sake of the business and perhaps a commission. No thanks!

It seems like unless I am a "professional"—meaning that I hold a degree in a specialized discipline, such as teaching or engineering—the only jobs for me are commission based or really just rather poor ones—not that all work isn't honorable as I have said, but you know what I mean. As an aside, I made more money teaching in Korea while working only half the time I need to work here at home—and we are a first-world country? Maybe I should go back to Asia. I am surely not going to try to get any of these jobs. It is weird that I am in the top 50 percent in the world when it comes to IQ, but my society has no jobs for me? This makes my blood boil.

As for education, how many people out there could possibly find the cure for cancer, for example, if properly educated but, because society does not equally take care of all its people, don't even get the chance to go to school and learn how to help others? I guess we can keep hoping that one of the 7 percent who actually have a college degree can figure that out. But who wants to bet on those odds? It is such a sad world that I want to drive over someone's toes to make myself feel better.

As for Korea, I did enjoy my time in Asia, but I encountered a few things I just couldn't get used to, the locals' eating habits to name one. Wow, they are loud eaters. Young, old, man, or woman; it didn't matter. I will not even get into gum chewing; forget about it. Really, being around others there while they were eating had to be like being next to a lion at a kill. People slurp and chomp everything—even beverages. I couldn't make so much noise if I tried. I should say here, as an aside, that this noisy eating style was an Asian thing and not solely the domain of South Korea. Anyway, thank goodness for my ear condoms. They protected me everywhere I went. I am referring to my iPod here.

I know I said that buying products like iPods is a waste of money, but mine is a one gig that my former partner bought for me because she was embarrassed when I took out my CD player. The CD player was over ten years old when I received my iPod, which is now going on five, and I still have both. Not bad I think. And for the record, the only reason I use my iPod is because people bother me and my senses, and the iPod helps me to tune them out.

I just hope no one's tracking me through my iPod use. I just read that iPhones and iPads have tracking devices in them and that Apple is storing this information somewhere. Why and where this information is being kept, who knows, but the possibility that it is makes me wonder how anonymous I really am. I know I am not totally free, but I don't know to what extent I am not. Cyber crooks like Murdoch can "steal" personal information from you, some sites will sell your private data to businesses, and new wonderful modes of technology now track my whereabouts. Where is my freedom—my right to anonymity?

I am being tracked on the Internet, and everywhere I turn now there is a camera looking at me like I'm guilty of something. My guess is the government has DNA profiles of everyone now as well. Next people will be have computer chips—which we'll be told will make our lives better and more convenient but will really be just a another tracking device to keep tabs on us—surgically implanted. We are not free, people, as much as we like to think we are. The noose is being pulled tighter every day.

Getting back to table manners, I am comparing the smacking professionals to what I consider is normal. But, obviously, what I deem to be standard may not be typical at all. When I was young, if I did anything wrong at the dinner table, it was off to my room for the night. Perhaps my teachings were a little stricter than most or maybe they were even way off the beaten path of what is normal, but that was my upbringing. Knowing this helps me to realize that it is conceivably me, not the "chompers," with the problem. People, no matter where they live, are just adhering to their own social norms, and this is okay.

I like Taiwan and Singapore. In Taiwan, you're not allowed to eat anything on the subway, and in Singapore, gum isn't allowed. In Korea, 90 percent of the people I encountered on the subway were chewing gum like they were out on a baseball diamond. In addition, they talked so loudly on the phone I could hear what was happening to the Kim's family six cars down. In conclusion, all I can say about this is enjoy your food, but please keep the sounds to yourself, you person you. Thank you.

All said and done, my search of the classified section hasn't been all for naught. I have found a couple of dead-end, life without parole, career jobs out of about two hundred listings that I could see myself possibly doing in the paper-without stabbing someone that is. I won't be happy at either of these jobs, but what can I do—assuming the stabbing part is a no for sure?

I look for a pen so I can jot down some information, but I don't have one, so off we go on the adventure of a lifetime; man, my life is boring. Sadly, this may just be the highlight of my day, though. Weird, though, that I say my life is boring when, before, I was hoping to be able to relax more and not work. Strange!

I peel myself off and out of "my" chair and set off in search of the elusive blue pen, once common but now rare in these parts of the jungle, now filled with laser ink. Man I am good! This was the icing on the cake for sure. I accept the "Sheikh Zayod Book Award" with great dignity and honor. Call me, Jawdat. Apt name for sure.

I have used a few odd names and words on this journey of ours, and I am hoping you took the time to look up everything you didn't know. Did you know, for example, that Toumai—a name I used earlier in reference to older people—is the nickname of the oldest humanoid ever discovered on Earth? Pretty cool or what! And for the record, the Zayod Book Award is real, as is the name Jawdat.

"Ouch! This is not good people. Sorry but we need to finish this story and quick!"

Off I go like a mouse in a maze in search of moldy cheese. Actually, getting some food is not a bad idea. I am so hungry right now. I make a deal with myself—I will eat sometime later. Even when negotiating with myself, I get severely grated.

I peer down the first of about thirty book-laden corridors but see no one. Murphy's Law in action—when you need one, no certified book dude is around, but when you want quiet, the bus carrying the kindergarten kids who are on a once-in-a-lifetime book tour is pulling into the parking lot.

While meandering about, I see the travel Afghanistan book again, and without thinking, I pick it up and randomly turn to page forty-eight. What I find there is not what I'd imagined. What a shock! The caves for sale are quite nice.

I think that the author of the *D-Day* book must have penned this Afghan travel guide as well. It's weird that, even though I still can't get my mind around the legitimacy of the *D-Day* book, I am enjoying it. Maybe in time, in an interesting thought that has come way too late, I could get used to seeing *D-Day* without thinking about war or anything bad like the author claimed he has. But the term *D-Day* always seems to be used when talking about something that is not pleasant doesn't it? Good luck with that.

Still looking for a pen, I walk past a few more deserted rows when, out of the blue, I catch, out of the corner of my eye, an apron-wearing, "book find person." The hunt is really on now. I push three kids who were playing tag aside and burn by a mother nursing her baby as I pursue my goal, oddly enough, with more determination than I did my last job. Anyway, I cruise around the corner, forgoing common sense—that slowing down and looking for someone else coming from the other direction is wise.

This reminds me of a time when I was shopping at the grocery store. I was looking for my partner when I whipped my cart and myself around the corner and the following happened:

"Aughhh!"

"I didn't see you. Are you okay?" I asked.

"Yes, I'm fine. Thank you."

"Okay. Be careful and have a good day," I said as I walked away.

"Thanks," he replied with a quizzical look on his face.

What a story! I let that situation slide even though the accident was my fault. Am I nice or what? He ended up the worst off, but I didn't say sorry; although, I feel sorry now. Of course, this is the point of that last story-feeling guilt.

It's weird that I carry around this feeling of guilt yet I don't carry around any hatred for others who were at fault for something they did to me. Everyone gets forgiven, except me. *Jamie, smarten up! Stop being so hard on yourself! Stop being so afraid! You have been down this street enough times already. You know exactly where this well-paved road goes—straight down.* I wish I'd talked to myself like this when I was healthier.

Having to rationalize your poor behavior just to feel somewhat comfortable with yourself (while, of course, still feeling terrible) is not the best line of attack behind which to live your life. I am so sad. I need to take evasive action and quickly before I start to cry again. I notice someone walking toward "my," chair so I decide to run back over to where it rests and regain my throne. Success…I start to whimper quietly as life around me begins to turn hectic.

FADE TO BLACK: THE GOOD-BYE

SO, WHAT WAS I talking about? Oh, yes, the activity of ignoring guilt, or CADD (convenient attention deficit disorder). I can't change the past, and I feel a bout of CADD coming on, so I guess I should take some synthetic pills for my terminal pain.

D-Day, please save me, I think, in an ironic twist of focus and reasoning. But I thought about this stunning turn of events, me actually wanting to read this book and find answers that could help me, no longer than it took to read it, and began reading for the last time.

I gazed passionately into her eyes. My soft hands caressed her breasts.

What the hell is this crap? I briefly think. And then I continue reading. I really do need to find some action soon, as my time is coming. Anyway, after a short time of quality mental masturbation, I begin to bore with the mannequin romance and, at the same time, yearn for my beloved *D-Day.* You get what you focus on and unconsciously so, good or bad!

I open the book randomly to page sixty-something but decide it is getting late. So heading home to relax, like my day has been stressful, pops into my mind like a sprouting weed in a neglected fruit garden. Let's go home, worry about not having a job or money coming in, and sleep as well as my short-term memory will allow.

I mosey up to the front when I remember the last time I was bipedal and ran into Bob here. The encounter went something like this.

"Hi, Bob. How are you?"

"Good, Jamie. I must say it's nice to see you out and about. How are you?"

207

"I think I'm doing okay, but how do I really know? How is your friend?"

"He's doing great, thanks. I actually got him a job at the hospital, so …"

For some, life goes on. Life stops for everyone at one point, of course, but until then, your time just keeps on ticking away. You now may be wondering how this story will end. Is there adventure? Is there romance? Does it end like a Shakespearean tragedy? Does the light within get to shine brightly?

Well, I will tell you this: I am in the ICU at the hospital. Actually, I have almost been here this whole time we have been talking. Look back—do you remember when I was in the shower and I called 9-1-1? Do you recall Bob coming up the driveway with purpose and cables, and getting strapped in for my ride to hell? Think about it—Heather and her white coat, and my constant desire to have done things differently in my life. This was my story, my life.

If you've made it this far, I imagine you enjoyed my purging romp through the world as I see it today. It would be cool if you could learn something from it on some level as well. That said, please think about everything I have talked about. There is a great deal more to this story than meets the eye. Not everything is as it seems. I wrote every word in this book with purpose, and I hope you understand that. I wish I could tell you more, but the path of life is yours to follow in any way you see fit. So do with my story what you will. Anyway, you now know my fate; what's yours?

It's time to end my nightmare. Only mental pictures of my loved ones are running through my mind now. I start to cry—freedom!

"I need more juice and a shot of epinephrine stat! Let's go! Clear!"

"Nothing, Heather!"

"Charge and clear!"

"He is still flat-lining! Dr. Heather, what do you think? It has been over ten minutes. Should we give Jamie another jump?"

"It doesn't look good, Nurse Bob. Call Pete and tell him we have another body here. Mark the time. I will notify his family," Heather states sadly.

"Tragic! He seemed like such a good person, too. I hope he is at peace now," Bob full-heartedly concludes.

"Okay, Bob. Who's next?"